EXETER MEDIEVAL ENGLISH TEXTS AND STUDIES

General Editors: Marion Glasscoe & M.J. Swanton

Amys and Amylion

Edited
by
FRANÇOISE LE SAUX

UNIVERSITY
of
EXETER
PRESS

First published in 1993 by
University of Exeter Press
Reed Hall
Streatham Drive
Exeter EX4 4QR
UK

British Library Cataloguing in Publication Data
A catalogue record for this book
is available from the British Library

Printed and bound by CPI Group (UK) Ltd, Croydon, CR0 4YY

CONTENTS

PREFACE

This volume is dedicated to my students at Lausanne University, whose enthusiasm for comparative approaches between French and English texts first alerted me to the absence on the market of an accessible edition of the English *Amys and Amylion*. I am indebted to them for many suggestions concerning the format of the book; the very detailed glossary and the inclusion of the etymologies of words is in direct response to the requirements expressed.

I wish to thank my colleagues of the English and Medieval French Departments of the University of Lausanne for their interest in my project. Special gratitude is moreover owed to Professor Michael Swanton, who encouraged me in my task; to Dr Marshal Grant, who helped me to solve a particularly worrying lexicographical problem; and to Dr Neil Wright, who generously shared his expertise in the field of classical and medieval Latin.

Lausanne, 1992   Françoise H.M. Le Saux

INTRODUCTION

A. The story

The story of Amys and Amylion was extremely popular throughout the Middle Ages.[1] Versions of it are found in Latin, French, English, Welsh, German, Flemish, Old Norse, and indeed, in most of the written vernaculars of medieval Europe. These versions include not only poetry and prose, but also drama, and a wide range of genres, from saint's life to *chanson de geste*, from miracle-play to secular romance.[2] This fascination is due to the fact that the story is a complex blend of myth, folk-tale, pious legend and historical anecdote, which provided potent material in an infinitely adaptable form.[3] The bare bones of the tale of Amys and Amylion read as follows.

Two youths who uncannily resemble each other are linked by an exceedingly strong friendship. During the absence of one of the friends, the other seduces the daughter of his lord. He is denounced and has to clear himself of the accusation in judicial combat. To avoid dishonour and certain death, the friends change places. While the one goes to fight, the other pretends to be his companion, even sharing his wife's bed, with whom however he refrains from having intercourse by placing a sword between them at night. The accuser is killed in battle, and, on resuming his true identity, the seducer marries the lord's daughter and eventually succeeds his father-in-law. Some time later, the other friend becomes a leper, and is rejected by his wife. After much suffering, he turns up as a beggar at the gates of the castle of his companion, who is now a great lord. The sick man is welcomed and nursed; then, hearing that the blood of children may cleanse his friend's leprosy, the lord kills his sons. The cure works, and the children are miraculously restored to life. The two friends are buried in Lombardy, united in death as they were in life.

Depending on the sensibilities of the different poets or redactors, more or less prominence was given to the various aspects of this plot. It is thus usual to distinguish between the so-called hagiographical versions —where the two heroes are not only characterised by their incomparable friendship, but also by their saintliness culminating in martyrdom— and the more secular versions,

---

[1] The names of the heroes are spelled as they first appear in our text, unless we are referring specifically to a different version of the work. References to the English poem are made by stanza and line; for example, 24:3 (= stanza 4, line 3).

[2] For a list of the main extant versions of the story, see LEACH, pp.ix-xiv.

[3] An analysis of the different levels of interpretation of the story is given by PLANCHE.

among which is numbered the English romance.[4] In all cases, however, the theme of the double is central, to the extent that certain texts invert the names of the heroes, who appear as truly indistinguishable; and supremely, it is the absolute nature of the bond between the heroes which is celebrated in these works. In order fully to appreciate the English *Amys and Aymlion*, it is therefore useful to have some knowledge of the major versions of the legend which predate it.

The oldest account we have of the adventures of Amis and his friend is in the Latin verse epistle "Ad Bernardum", by the eleventh-century poet Rodulfus Tortarius, summarized in Appendix 1.[5] The story, which covers 203 of the 340 lines of "Ad Bernardum", is given as an *exemplum* of friendship; it appears after other *exempla* taken from classical mythology, and is recounted as a fable which, though well-known, is not entirely trustworthy: *Vera tamen falsis quaedam permixta uidentur* (line 121), "However, true elements appear to be mingled with the false". Moreover, the *cauda* to the story suggests that Rodulfus may be presenting it as a counter-example to illustrate excessive friendship, rather than to provide a model. The epistle continues (lines 321-4):

> Haec retuli tibi, care mihi, studeas ut amari,
> Pro sola spernas id modo iustitia:
> Iusticiae zelo licet irasci tibi caro,
> Maior amicicia denique iusticia

"I have told you this, my dear, in order that you be intent on being loved, spurning it only for justice: for justice's sake you may be angry with a friend, for justice is greater than friendship".

Rodulfus's attitude towards the tale is therefore more complex than is generally recognised. The literary sub-text to the epistle is likewise richer than a cursory glance would suggest. The seemingly minor detail of Roland's sword given by the heroine to her champion firmly links Rodulfus's summary with both the hagiographical and the secular versions: Durandal, according to the *Chanson de*

---

[4] The relationship between the hagiographical and secular aspects in given texts are analysed by LEACH, pp.xiv-xxii and by HUME:1970. The term "romantic" frequently fiven to the non-hagiographical versions is misleading, since a number of these texts would better qualify as epic.

[5] On Rodulfus Tortarius and his work, see RABY vol.2, pp.23-26, and MANITIUS, vol.3, pp.872-77. The standard edition of the epistles of Rodulfus Tortarius is by OGLE and SCHULLIAN: an English paraphrase of "Ad Bernardum" is provided in the introduction, pp.xv-xvi, and the Latin text is on pp.266-7. An English translation of the section of "Ad Bernardum" relating the story of Amicus and Amelius may moreover be found in LEACH (Appendix A, pp.101-105).

2

Roland (lines 2318-21) was given to Charlemagne by an angel, to pass on to one of his vassals. The duel of Amicus is thus endowed with both heroic and religious connotations.

The religious aspect is given more prominence in the twelfth-century Latin prose *Vita Amici et Amelii carissimorum*, of which a summary may be found in Appendix 2.[6] As compared to "Ad Bernardum", it is characterized by the total absence of any doubt as to the veracity or the didactic value of the narrative, which now has an openly hagiographical status, since after their adventures the two heroes die in odour of sanctity. Moreover, the account is given a heightened prestige through the explicit presence of Charlemagne among the *dramatis personae*. The *Vita* thus reads as a doubly authoritative text, both by the integration of themes and features proper to the saint's life such as angels, demons, baptism and martyrdom, and by its absorbtion into the supposedly historically-based "Matter of France".

The carolingian setting recurs in the French *chanson de geste Ami et Amile*, written around 1200. This, of all the versions of the story the most studied by modern critics, is summarized in Appendix 3.[7] As in the *Vita*, the friendship of the heroes starts in infancy, with their baptism at Rome by the Pope himself, who gives them identical cups. However, the *chanson* takes less interest in the heroes' warlike qualities —their campaigning with Charlemagne is not recounted— whilst the religious aspect is more subtly expressed by making the protagonists search for each other at great length on the major medieval pilgrimage routes. A number of more specifically epic themes appear, like that of the evil lineage; the accuser who exposes the seduction of Charlemagne's daughter is thus said to be related to Ganelon, the traitor in the *Chanson de Roland*, as is the merciless wife who rejects leprous Ami. Yet at the same time the *chanson de geste* gives unusual prominence to female characters, a trait usually connected with romance rather than epic: this is indicative of the flexibility of the narrative tradition of the story.

Roughly contemporaneous with the *chanson de geste* is the Anglo-Norman romance *Amys e Amillyoun*, which of all the extant versions of the story, is the closest to the English poem.[8] It has come down to us in three

---

[6] The only edition of this work is in KÖLBING, pp.xcvii-cx.

[7] The standard edition is that of DEMBOWSKI; a good survey of the relationship of the *chanson* with the Latin texts may be found in MENARD.

[8] These three manuscripts are: Cambridge, Corpus Christi College, MS 50 (second half of 13th century), London, British Library, MS Royal 12.C XII (end of 13th/beginning of 14th century) and Karlsruhe, Badische Landesbibliothek, MS 345 (end of 14th century). The Cambridge and London texts are very close; the Karlsruhe text stands apart, to the extent of constituting another version of the poem. The London text is edited by

manuscripts, the oldest of which dates from the second half of the thirteenth century; a summary of the earliest of these texts may be found in Appendix 4. The salient feature of the romance is its relative brevity: written in octosyllabic couplets, it is almost three times shorter than the *chanson*, which comprises 3504 decasyllabic lines. Instead of the carolingian setting, we find ourselves in a historically unspecified period; even the lord who fosters and trains the heroes remains nameless. The devotional dimension appears as an afterthought in the last ten lines of the poem, yet it is styled a *sermoun* (line 1240) in the conclusion, in what appears to be an attempt to reconcile versions of the story displaying different narrative priorities. Awareness of conflicting traditions is also signalled by the twice-made distinction between the habitual and the real name of a character: the heroine is called Florie, but her real name is Mirabele, Amillyoun's faithful servant is called Amoraunt but his real name is Owein. That the Amys and Amylion story was subjected to considerable *mouvance*, and that the different narrative traditions were in a constant dialogue, is finally demonstrated by the existence of the Karlsruhe text of the Anglo-Norman romance (in the latest of the three manuscripts), which integrates into the work features derived from the *chanson de geste*, thus creating yet another, distinctive version of the story. It is in the light of such fluctuations that the English *Amys and Aymlion* is most fruitfully read.

B. The English *Amys and Amylion*

1. Plot and Characterization.

Compared to its ancestor the Anglo-Norman romance, the English *Amys and Amylion* has a number of characteristic features which change the whole import of the story. These are partly due to the transference from French into English, which made the names of the main characters meaningless whereas in the Latin and French versions the heroes' names were self-explanatory. Amys especially must have posed problems, since his name no longer fulfilled the emblematic function it had for the original French audience: to the English ear, the name Amys might suggest sin rather than friendship, a character who goes amiss, rather than a friend. Equally, the similarity of the names of the heroes (in French, the stress in both Ami and Amiles is on the *i*), which underlined and confirmed their resemblance, is less striking in English; the theme of physical resemblance, though important, and indeed essential for the substitution episode, is accordingly given less emphasis. The English texts are the only ones to suggest that Belesawnt could distinguish between the two men, whose background appears moreover to be somewhat differentiated: both

---

FUKUI, from which all quotations will be made; the only critical edition available is KÖLBING, pp.111-187.

are born of barons, but of Amylion only are we told more explicitly that he was *of grete renoun* and *Ycomen of hye ospryng* (4:11-12). To this one may add that positive epithets occur slightly more frequently in connection with Amylion than with Amys, whose behaviour during most of the narrative confirms the negative aspect hinted at by his name.[9] Amylion may thus be said to be the true hero in the English versions; and it is striking that the sin which brings the curse of leprosy upon him is no longer bigamy —which may be read as an echo of Amys's unchaste behaviour with his lord's daughter— but rather Amylion's contempt for God's justice through not revealing his true identity before the battle.[10] This change in the English texts, which could be considered as a mere anticipation of Amylion's vision, is in fact closely linked with Belesawnt's knowledge of the true identity of her champion in this version of the story. In the French versions, the prospective bride has no such knowledge, and the wedding is rushed; in the *chanson de geste*, Charlemagne refuses to let the hero leave the court before giving his solemn oath to marry the girl, while in the Anglo-Norman romance the marriage takes place immediately after the fight. In the English romance, Belesawnt's awareness of the identity of Amylion, linked with the realistic detail of having to tend Amylion's wounds, allows the heroes to resume their rightful places before the wedding, and thus removes the theme of bigamy entirely. As a result, the bedroom scene we find in the Anglo-Norman romance between Amylion and Florie during their wedding-night, which forms a parallel with Amys's equally chaste nights with Amylion's wife, also disappears. This suggests an imbalance in the virtue of the two friends, since Amylion's sexuality is depicted as totally honourable, in contrast with Amys's illicit liaison with Belesawnt, and the hint of concupiscence contained in his brusqueness towards Amylion's wife. The confession made to Florie in order to avoid consummating a marriage contracted in his friend's name is, moreover, replaced by Amylion's confession to his own wife on his return, which further links the character with legitimate sexuality.

---

[9] KRAMER, p.113, is of the opinion that Belesawnt and her mother would not have noticed the substitution had they not been forewarned; however, the absence of any mention in the English poem that Belesawnt might have confused the two men is surely relevant. In the French texts, the confusion is explicitly stated twice: during the substitution and after the leper's cure. Moreover, the structural argument advanced by HUME:1973, pp.25-6, in favour of the equality of the heroes, ignores the fact that most of the narrative focusses on Amylion, and that Amys only appears in a positive light from stanza 172 onwards.

[10] KRATINS and DANNENBAUM consider that the angel's warning is morally neutral and free from any suggestion of sin on the hero's part. In view of the medieval literary tradition of leprosy, this is unlikely. See BRODY, REMY or PICHON.

The disappearance of the theme of bigamy and the toning down of the interchangeable nature of the heroes has as corollary a renewed emphasis on the theme of *trewthe*.[11] The angel's warning to Amylion, which occurs before the battle rather than the wedding, links the hero's leprosy to his perversion of God's justice, and justifies to a great extent the reaction of Amylion's wife when she hears of his role in the judicial combat: *With wrong and with unryght / Thou slew there a dowty knyght: / It was well evell ydo!* (122:4-6). It is noteworthy that the theme of *trewthe* is also prominent in the *chanson de geste*, where almost every decision taken by the characters is to some extent foreshadowed by a previous oath, as for example when Belissant vows on her wedding-day never to come between the two friends: this precludes any negative reaction on her part to the welcoming of the leper Ami or the slaying of her children. In the English romance, *trewthe* is given a strong moral and religious resonance from the beginning of the poem, where Jesus is explicitly said to have rewarded Amys and Amylion because they were *trewe in alle thing* (3:10). Loyalty to one's word, more so than in the Anglo-Norman romance, thus becomes the chief virtue both in heaven and on earth. On the level of characterisation, it is also the distinguishing quality between heroes and villains.

The steward is in all versions of the tale the arch-villain. In the *chanson de geste*, the treachery of Hardré is inherent in his personality: he is related to the traitor Ganelon, who betrayed Roland at Roncevaux, and his blood is bad. His animosity against the heroes appears to be due to nothing other than their essential goodness, and he shows the extent of his depravity during the judicial combat by revealing his allegiance to the devil rather than to God. Neither the Anglo-Norman nor the English versions retain these two traits; as a result, the death of the seneschal/steward during a duel where he is in the right becomes somewhat problematic.[12] The English poem attempts to attenuate the injustice of the steward's end by stressing his perverse desire to dishonour Amys, and his particularly unsavoury voyeurism, which makes him observe the lovers through a peep-hole — in the Anglo-Norman romance he does not stoop that far. Moreover, both the Anglo-Norman and the English versions retain the steward's vindictiveness against the heroine and her mother, the queen —an indirect way perhaps of indicating a latent animosity against his lord— and contrast it with Amylion's benign wit when he counters the order to burn

---

[11] On the importance of the theme, see BALDWIN and KRATINS.

[12] See MICKEL's perceptive analysis of the problematics surrounding the judicial combat; also LEGROS and (more specifically on the issue of religion in the French *chanson*) MADIKA.

the ladies with *Yt were moche unryght to make roste of ladyes bryght!*[13] However, in parallel, Amys's blunt rejection of the steward's offer of friendship clearly reads as the objective starting-point of the enmity between the two men.

The reasons for this rejection are twofold. First, of course, Amys has been warned against the steward by Amylion; but this warning is less strong in the English romance, which puts a greater stress on the way the steward's offer is couched. We are not talking of friendship as much as a proposal to Amys to change his personal priorities —*Y schall be to the a better frend than ever ryght was he* — and violate the oath of absolute loyalty given to Amylion. The relationship between the two heroes in this passage is reminiscent of that of lovers; Amys's answer *Y schall never, be nyght ne day, chonge him for no newe* (31:11-12) is strikingly similar to Belesawnt's demand to Amys that he *never chaunge for no newe that in this world ys born* (48:8-9). The steward is thus the odd-one-out in a process of male bonding that is as exclusive and absolute as that of sexual attachment.[14] Despite the steward's supposed power and authority, and through no obvious fault of his own, he is excluded from the restricted circle with which the reader is meant to identify.

The problem remains, however, that the steward is consistently called a traitor by those who have best reason to know that his accusation is perfectly correct. This suggests that just as Amylion's breach of *trewthe* was compatible with human rules (even if this is only so through a ruse), so too the steward's treachery may be. This hypothesis gains in strength if one considers that the steward's actions are only superficially positive. His offer of friendship to Amys, in full knowledge of his prior commitment to Amylion, may be read as a conscious attempt to seduce Amys into disloyalty. Similarly, his jubilant eagerness to denounce the lovers betrays his unconcern for his lord's honour: he is fundamentally a *trewthe*-less vassal. Finally, his lack of compassion towards Amys's pledges shows him up as totally heartless. All this mounts up to a villain with a relish for evil that may truly be termed diabolical, but expressed in such a way that it is in harmony with the letter, if not the spirit, of the law.[15]

This dichotomy between human rules and the reader's response to the behaviour of an apparently law-abiding character recurs in connection with the other villain of the poem, Amylion's wife. The contradiction is less obvious in

---

[13] 101:10-11; cp. *Trop vileine roste serreit!* (FUKUI, line 570). This *mot d'esprit* is proper to the "romance" versions of the story. In the *chanson de geste*, the hero's pledges are to be beheaded.

[14] Many observations made by KAY on the subject (in connection with the *chanson*) remain valid for our text.

[15] KRATINS (p.351) speaks in this connection of a conflict between "a higher and lower justice".

her case than in that of the steward, mainly because the contemporary reader naturally has little sympathy with the discrimination medieval society inflicted upon lepers. The tension, however, is real, and it is discretely underlined in the English romance by explicit references to social pressure and legal dispositions which influence the attitude of different characters towards the leper Amylion. The hero's nameless wife thus justifies her decision to banish her sick husband from court by referring to public opinion: *Yef in my lond spring that worde Y fede a lazar at my borde that is so foule a thing, it is grete spite to a ladys kende* (129:7-10), and *It ys grete spite to us all that thou hast ben so long in hall. My kynne ys wroth with me* (130:4-6). These words are less harsh and hypocritical than they appear. At this stage, Amylion has been a leper for six months, a long time for a man suffering from what was considered a highly contagious illness to remain in society, and the decision to seclude him in a *pryve logge* was right and proper according to the customs of the time.[16] As with the steward, the sin committed by Amylion's wife is a breach of the *trewthe* she owes to her husband by virtue of her marriage vows: her subsequent refusal to feed him, then her intended remarriage, though probably not an unusual occurrence in everyday medieval experience, reveals the moral weakness of her character. However, her rejection of her husband is clearly motivated by moral reasons: she reads Amylion's leprosy as divine punishment for the terrible sin he committed in killing the steward. Moreover, Amylion's substitution trick put her in danger of unwittingly committing adultery, as well as betraying the limits of his commitment towards her and their marriage.

The situation in the French versions is somewhat different, in that the hero's wife never learns of the substitution, and therefore lacks that particular motivation for her harshness. In the Anglo-Norman romance, the character is particularly hazy from that point of view; she appears to be pointlessly cruel in her rejection of her husband, and is shown up as being cowardly as well as faithless at Amillyoun's return, since she attempts to avoid seeing him after his cure and thinks of entering a convent to escape from him altogether. Her fears are amply justified, since she is walled in a stone tower as punishment: a fate seen as exemplary by the poet. The Lubias of the *chanson de geste* is more interesting. First, she has a name and a family: Lubias is the niece of the traitor Hardré. She is not told of the substitution that makes her husband the slayer of her kinsman, but she is nevertheless a spurned woman, threatened by the excessive friendship of Ami and Amiles: she was first offered in marriage to Amiles, but he gave her (and her ample possessions) to Ami. The relationship between Lubias and Ami appears to be passionate, and the couple have a son, whereas they are childless in the other versions we are considering

---

[16] See BRODY, esp. pp.60-106.

8

here.[17] Similarly, the *chanson* stands out from the Anglo-Norman and the English romances in having the husband forbid his friend to touch Lubias (*Li siens services voz iert abandonnéz, Sire compains, et voz le refuséz*, "Her attentions will be within your reach, my lord companion, but refuse them", lines 1088-9) during the substitution. Moreover, when Ami returns to Blaye, Lubias is not about to remarry, as in the romances, but offers her person to him as a peace-offering, and his punishment of her only lasts eight days, then she is reinstated. This happy end for the villainess is all the more striking for the explicit condemnation of the character repeatedly expressed by the narrator, by Ami himself and, most forcibly, by the bishop whom Lubias tries to bribe and intimidate into declaring her separated from her husband. When Lubias offers thirty pounds to him to free her from the leper, he declares (lines 2125-9):

> Dex, dist l'evesques, qui onques ne mentis,
> Biaus tres douz Dex, merveilles puis oïr!
> Se touz li mondes le pensast et jehist,
> Sel deüssiéz et celer et couvrir
> Conme la dame qui l'avoit a mari

"'God who never lied', said the bishop, 'beautiful and most sweet God, what a wonder I have heard! Even if the whole world suspected and denounced it, you should have hidden and concealed the fact, as befitting the lady who had him for husband.'"

Lubias eventually gets her own way by bribing the townsfolk into denouncing her husband's leprosy, and further shows her evil nature by throwing her son into prison to stop him from helping his father.

The character in the two romances thus stands somewhat apart from the *chanson*'s Lubias. Amylion's wife, in her anonymity, epitomizes the essential non-existence of any bond between the couple. For Amylion, marriage is of secondary importance, on both the emotional and moral level; his wife is an object which can be lent to his friend, and destroyed when it no longer satisfies. The romances display a subtle interplay of double standards for Amylion and his wife, which only the confession scene in the English poem prevents from becoming intrusive. Amylion's admission of the substitution gives the reader the illusion of the hero's *trewthe* towards his wife, which is then implicitly contrasted with her own refusal of conjugal solidarity and love.

---

[17] In the Karlsruhe version of the Anglo-Norman romance, however, the couple also have a son, who is killed by his mother for having visited his leprous father.

9

The tension between common-sense duty and more intimate moral requirements is not restricted to villains. It also appears prominently in the character of Belesawnt, who in all versions is depicted favourably, yet may be convicted of lechery, vicarious perjury and connivance in infanticide. She is a completely amoral character, with only one guiding principle: blind loyalty towards the husband gained by foul means rather than fair. This unquestioning *trewthe* of Belesawnt is of course to be contrasted with the critical response of Amylion's wife to his misdeeds; it is however noteworthy that the positive woman in the story is the one who denies herself any independent thought or desire, to the extent of condoning the murder of her own children. Belesawnt's choices apparently all run counter to honour and basic morality: she blackmails Amys into becoming her lover; when found out, she resorts to lies, and does her utmost to counter justice; and finally she approves of the sacrifice of her children in order to cure her husband's friend.[18] Yet, inasmuch as these choices derive from a love for Amys as inordinate as that linking the two heroes, they are seen as permissible, and indeed laudable. Belesawnt is to some extent a feminine version of Amylion, giving precedence to her loyalty over and above all other social or moral considerations, and supporting him in *wrong and ryght*.[19]

The English romance thus reads as a secularized saint's life, where the options taken by the villains, though intuitively correct, are discredited as being worldly, superficial and evil, while those taken by the heroes, though dubious, are presented as superior and divinely inspired. The work tones down the openly hagiographic element, but extolls the ideal of absolute and exclusive loyalty towards another human being, to the extent that on the literal level the poem smacks somewhat of blasphemy. With the weakening of the passive symbolism contained in the Latin and French forms of the names of the main characters, the abstract exemplum of friendship and devotion becomes a glorification of private values to the potential detriment of social harmony.

This subversive element is however attenuated by the "folk-tale" dimension of the story. That a number of themes may be traced back ultimately to folk motifs has been pointed out by a number of critics;[20] to this one may add that

---

[18] These negative traits are even more prominent in the *chanson de geste*, where Belissant deceives Amile into thinking he is sleeping with a chambermaid, and where (as in the Anglo-Norman romance) she does not know that her champion is not her lover, and therefore not guilty of perjury; the darker aspects of the character are perceptively analysed by ROSENBERG.

[19] This expression, which is quoted in the text as the terms of the heroes' oath of brotherhood (13:5), sums up quite adequately the attitude the narrator also expects of the wives in the poem.

[20] See for example LEACH, pp.xxxii-lxv, HUET or KRAPPE, for whom the story is "an ancient Dioscuric myth" (p.161).

as in the folk-tale, the English romance presents an extremely simplified world-view. This is most obvious in the treatment of the character of Amys. After having destabilised the social structure through his seduction of Belesawnt and reestablished it by succeeding her father, he loses whatever identity he may have had to become a double of the former duke. The scene where Amys recognises Amylion's cup thus echoes the duke's discovery of his daughter's dishonour: both fly into a fury of outrage and attempt to kill the supposed criminal before bothering to enquire further. Similarly, the duke's readiness to execute Belesawnt may be seen as parallel to Amys's killing of his children; in both cases, the sense of duty overcomes natural feelings. In this respect, Amys may be recognised as a type to a greater extent than his counterpart in the French analogues, where the heroine's father retains some amount of self-control. The overall structure of the story, with its double transgression leading to adventures which, when solved, restore harmony, is equally reminiscent of the characteristics of the folk-tale as defined by Vladimir Propp. The warped moral stance of the narrator becomes acceptable in such a context, since we are implicitly adopting the folk-tale outlook whereby the hero is ensured of the audience's sympathy whatever he does.

However, romances are not folk-tales, and the true key to the poem's discourse lies elsewhere, in the apparently minor character of Oweys. The institution that comes under the greatest threat in *Amys and Amylion* as in *Amys e Amillyoun* is clearly the family: the heroes substitute sworn brotherhood for blood-ties, and allow their oath to take precedence over both marriage and parentage. As pointed out by Dean Baldwin, in order to keep their *trewthe* to each other, the heroes accept to be disloyal, thus showing the moral and practical limitations of the bond uniting them. By contrast, Oweys is untrammelled by oaths, but his loyalty to Amylion is exemplary. Far more than a variation on the type of the faithful servant, Oweys may be said to represent the superiority of family ties —he is Amylion's nephew— over the type of relationship exemplified by the heroes. He requires no oath to remain true to his uncle, and thus remains free to act according to his conscience; which indeed he does, when he divulges the identity of the beggar to Amys despite having been forbidden to do so.

For all its apparent simplicity, *Amys and Amylion* is thus a poem of great richness. The heroes are sinners through their excessive attachment to a single virtue, and only a miracle averts the sinister ending prefigured by the murder of the children. Yet, despite everything, they find grace in the eyes of God for this one virtue they held above all others and which, more than loyalty in the strict sense of the word, may be understood as love. For, as the Anglo-Norman poet announces in his very first line, the poem is a *chaunzon d'amur*.

2. Versification

In all the extant manuscripts, the English *Amys and Amylion* is written in twelve-line tail-rhyme stanzas, a metre common to a number of English romances. The rhyme scheme of each stanza is aabaabccbddb; only very few stanzas in our text do not respect this pattern, generally due to an obvious corruption. However, the reader must make allowances for scribal peculiarities which may mask the rhyme; for example, 94:12, where we find *twoo* instead of the expected *tway*; or 144:3 and 6, where *gon* and *more* are best read *goo* and *moo*. The dozen or so cases of assonance rather than strict rhyme may equally be due to some extent to the various layers of scribal and dialectal influence, as in 129:3 or 176:7-8, where *drink* rhymes with *lesyng*.

In tail-rhyme stanzas, lines 1,2,4,5,7,8,10 and 11 have four stresses, and lines 3,6,9 and 12 have three. However, our text has a relatively high number of "defective" lines bearing three stresses instead of four (approximately one in 80 lines), predominantly in the second half of the poem. This could be due simply to scribal error, but one may note that these lines often occur at turning-points in the narrative, or at moments of heightened tension. It is therefore possible that in certain cases we are dealing with a deliberate device. This is especially likely in stanza 116, where we have an unusual succession of three-stress lines (9-12) reporting Amylion's refusal to be escorted home after his victory over the steward; and also in stanza 185:9-12, where the swifter tempo mirrors Amys's haste to get out of the nursery after his murder of the children. Similarly, in the context of speeches, the isolated "defective" lines give special emphasis to the feelings expressed by the characters: for example, the steward's outrage (69:10), the authority of the voice from heaven (103:5), or the assertiveness of the courtier describing Oweys' beauty (159:7).[21]

The metre is of the individual line is very fluid. Most lines have a basically iambic rhythm, with occasional "dips" of two or even three successive unstressed syllables; these "dips" occur at the beginning of the line (see 185:12) and within it, but never at the end. Trochaic rhythms are frequent (see 1:9), and though it is difficult to provide definite figures in these matters due to the flexibility of the metrical system of our poem, one may say that approximately one line in four starts with an initial stressed syllable. The four-stress lines have a caesura, which may be more or less marked, after the second stress; and one may note that in some lines the two halves often display what appear to be totally different rhythmical patterns (for example, 44:2). Leach (p.xcix) notes that the occasional addition of an unstressed syllable frequently improves the rythm of many such lines; this is certainly the case in the text

---

21 However, a comparison with the other texts also frequently suggests straightforward error, especially when the defective line is the first of a stanza.

edited here, where the scribe did not always bother to write down vowels weakened to schwa, even if it is most likely that they were pronounced. This trait is especially obvious in the spelling of the name of the heroine, which has to carry two stresses if the lines in which it appears are to be complete, yet is repeatedly written Belsaunt.[22] However, this does not account for all the stress clashes (i.e. two stressed syllables in succession) of the poem, and it is reasonable to assume that we are dealing here with a legitimate metrical device. It is striking, for example, that the clash between the first and the second stress of a line occurs mainly after a verb introducing speech (either reported or direct), thus functioning as a rhythmical marker (see 52:4 or 94:7).

The stanza is almost invariably a self-contained unit; in all the poem we find only two exceptions to this, stanzas 75 and 118, which continue the final sentences of 74 and 117. Enjambement from one line to another within a stanza is equally rare, to the extent of suggesting a scribal error, as is certainly the case in 86:11. The plot-advancing elements are generally contained in the four-stress lines; the three-stress lines (or tails) usually underline former statements with conventional alliterating formulae.[23] These alliterative formulaic expressions are the most important single narrative device in the poem. As noted, they occur predominantly in the three-stress lines of the stanza, but they are also frequently used in the longer lines to provide the final rhyme. The conventional nature of these expressions does not, however, mean that they can be dismissed as mere line-fillers. Their recurrence allows the formation of a nexus of connotations which invites comparison and lends additional depth to a poem characterized by narrative economy. The presence or absence of a given alliterating formula may thus be of some import when analysing characterization in the romance, for example.[24]

Another feature which must be mentioned here is the prominence given to the characters' verbal presence through a particularly lavish use of direct speech, which occurs in almost half of the stanzas and over 30% of the lines of the

---

[22] In two cases (35:8 and 114:7) the unstressed syllable appears in the spelling of the heroine's name, possibly because these lines were felt by the scribe as being at greater risk than the others of being misread (rhythmically speaking). In 35:8 in particular, without the extra syllable, the line would have ended with three successive stressed syllables, a feature apparently not allowed by the poem's metre.

[23] A list of these formulae may be found in KÖLBING, pp.xlii-lix. On the use of these formulae in tail-rhyme romances and on the aesthetic principles governing the stanza, see DÜRMÜLLER, pp.71-114; also WITTIG, pp.12-46.

[24] See DÜRMÜLLER, pp.97-105, on the function of such "stock phrases" in *The Erl of Tollous*.

poem.[25] In a few cases (for example stanzas 52 or 155), the effect of the direct speech passages is reinforced by preceding reported speech; if one adds the occasional use by the poet of free indirect style to echo the words or thoughts of different characters, the dramatic nature of his verse is even more apparent.

3. The Language of *Amys and Amylion*

Amys and Amylion is composed in an East Midlands dialect, with a varying number of Northern traits depending on the manuscript considered.[26] Kölbing, in his detailed analysis of the language of the romance, thus concludes that the work must have first been written on the northern border of the East Midlands. The manuscript with which we are more specially concerned displays late Midlands scribal traits.[27] A number of Northern forms are replaced, even at the rhyme: *ying*, for example, rhyming with *king*, *thing* or *lesing*, consistently becomes *yong* (53:4, 140:10, 158:9, 180:2). Similarly, present participles end in *-ing* rather than the Northern *-and*.

The following grammatical characteristics may briefly be mentioned. The infinitive of verbs is mainly in *-(e)*, and more rarely in *-n*. The two forms coexist in a handful of common verbs such as *do/don, fonde/fonden, have/han, sey/seyn*, etc. The infinitive is frequently identical in form with the imperative, the present tense, and even the subjunctive; *abyde* may thus denote either the infinitive, imperative or indicative present. Past participles occasionally display the perfective particle *y-/i-*, such as *ysene* (127:6), or *ibrought* (152:11). The most common personal endings are *-est* and *-eth*, for the second and third person singular, in the present tense. One may also note the ending *-eth/yth* for the plural imperative, as in *herkneth* (1:2), *herkenyth* (2:12). In the verb "to be" Northern and Midlands forms stand side by side: inf.: *ben(e)/be(e)/bien*; 1 sing. pres.: *am*; 2 sing pres., *art(e)/beth*; 3 sing. pres.: *is/ys*; pl. pres.: *was*; sing.p.: *was/wes*; pl.p.: *wes/ware(n)/were*; p.part.: *(y)ben*. The personal pronouns are the following:

	Nom.	Obl.	Poss.
1 sing.	I	me	my/myn/myne
2 sing.	thou/thow(e)	the	thi/thin/thyn
3 sing. fem.	sche/she	her(e)/hire	her(e)/hire

---

[25] This importance of direct speech is in keeping with the observations made by critics on other Middle English romances. DÜRMÜLLER (p.224) notes that certain tail-rhyme romances have over 70% of direct speech.
[26] However, H also presents a number of south-western features. See KÖLBING, pp.xxiv-xxxvii.
[27] That is, MS D. See below, pp.15-16.

3 sing. masc.	he	him/hym	his/hes
3 sing. neuter	(h)yt, (h)it	yt/it	his
1 pl.	we(e)	us	ure
2 pl.	ye	you/yow	
3 pl.	thei	(t)hem/him	(t)her(e)

Adjectives are in effect invariable, with the occasional addition of a functionless final -e. In nouns, we find three case-endings: -e, -n and -s. Final -s is the usual mark for the plural and the possessive forms. The text offers only few examples of an s-less plural: yen (96:2, etc.), childeryn (1:10, etc.), yere (5:7, etc.), to which one may add hors (14:11, etc.). Similarly, genitive forms without the final -s are rare: lady (199:5), suster (132:8), and heven(e) in the compound-like (Jhesu) heven king (3:11, etc.).

On the level of syntax, one may note the presence in this text of impersonal constructions such as him/here thought, "it seemed to him/her" (39:8, 83:4, etc.), and the poet's occasional use of parenthetical clauses, which are likely at times to pose problems, as for example in stanza 8. Elliptical constructions where the subject of a clause or the main verb remains implicit also crop up periodically (see for example 87:6). Such lines are glossed in the textual notes.

As one may gather from this brief outline, the language of the poem presents relatively few difficulties, even for the inexperienced reader. Most of the problems arise rather from the unnormalised spelling of the text. An inorganic -t occasionally appears at the end of certain words such as "though", spelled variously thoght, thaught, or "enough", spelled ynought; -ht is occasionally inverted, as in brouth for brouht, wrouth for wrouht; and th /d/t sometimes seem to be used interchangeably, as for example in 39:6, where kyde, elsewhere (102:2, 194:2) written kythe, is made to rhyme with lythe, blyth and sythe. The form tryve (58:12) alongside thryve (5:1, 141:12) may also be noted. It has therefore seemed useful to include all the variant forms of any given word in our text in the glossary.

C. The Texts of *Amys and Amylion*

1. Manuscripts

The Middle English *Amys and Amylion* is preserved in four manuscripts:

A   Edinburgh, National Library of Scotland, MS Auchinleck W.4.1. (Adv. 19.2.1), fos. 48d-61a.

S   London, British Library, MS Egerton 2862, fos. 135a-147c.

D   Oxford, Bodleian Library, MS Douce 326 (Bodleian 21900), fos. 1-13.

H   London, British Library, MS Harley 2386, fos. 131a-137d and 138.

A: *Auchinleck* is a parchment quarto of 334 pages dating from the first half of the fourteenth century; it is one of the major collections of Middle English romances.[28] It contained large illuminations which were torn or cut away by "collectors"; as a result, the text of *Amys and Amylion*, with a number of other pieces of this manuscript, has been mutilated at its beginning and end. The first 52 lines of the poem are lost, as also the first half of lines 53 to 94. Similarly, over a hundred lines are lost at the end of the poem, due to the loss of an illustration on the other side of the page. The unmutilated text starts at stanza 9:1, and ends with 192:8. This manuscript is generally thought to contain the best version of the English *Amys and Amylion*; the poem is somewhat longer than in other manuscripts, with six stanzas that are not attested in either S, D or H. Only one stanza, found in S and D, (stanza 170, Leach lines 2113-25) was omitted by the scribe.

S: *Egerton 2862*, also known as Duke of Sutherland after one of its previous owners, is a vellum manuscript of the end of the fourteenth century.[29] It originally comprised 148 pages, fourteen of which have now been lost, and contains seven items, all of them English romances. *Amys and Amylion* is the sixth of these. The loss of two folios at some stage in the history of the manuscript leaves a gap in the poem after line 1853 in Leach's text (between stanzas 149:4 and 176 of this edition).

D: *Douce 326* is a paper manuscript of vii + 22 leaves, dating from the second half of the fifteenth century. It contains two texts, of which *Vita de Amys and Amylion* is the first; this is the most complete version of the English poem, preserving 2395 out of a maximum possible total of 2508 lines for the work.[30] D is the manuscript edited here.

H: *Harley 2386* is a paper quarto of the fifteenth century containing a variety of material in different hands.[31] It is a compilation containing Latin pieces, household accounts, recipes against common ailments, Mandeville's Travels and last, stanzas 1-74:2 and 85:5-89:2 of *Amys and Amylion*.

---

[28] For a detailed description of this manuscript, see KÖLBING, "Vier Romanzen-Handschriften".

[29] For a description of this manuscript, see LEACH, pp.xci-ii.

[30] This manuscript is generally considered to be inferior to A or S; LEACH (pp.xcii-xciii), describes it in the following terms: "The scribe misread his copy occasionally, and he had other careless habits, such as reversing lines and repeating lines. There is no punctuation; no attempt to mark stanzas either by indentation or by the marginal mark". This is true; however, these shortcomings are by no means uncommon. The handwriting is clear, and scribal misreadings are generally of minor importance.

[31] See LEACH, pp.xciii-xciv.

The textual transmission of the poem has been studied by MacEdward Leach, who came to the conclusion that A was probably closest to the first English redaction of the poem; that H was at one remove from A; and that S and D were copied from the same (lost) manuscript one step further still from the "original" work. This must be viewed with some scepticism. The few variant readings of H which are not minor do not give any clear indication as to the exact relationship of the manuscript to the other remaining witnesses. Moreover, the Latin and French traditions from which the poem is derived are so complex that it is difficult to assign priority to one version or the other on the basis of contents only.[32] Even the A text, generally deemed to be the version closest to that of the "original" poem, is not above suspicion. The manuscript was an expensive one, and efforts appear to have been made to ensure that the text be as agreeable to read as possible: the additional stanzas in the manuscript, which are unattested elsewhere and are generally very trite, could be due to an "improving" scribe. Auchinleck is certainly the oldest extant manuscript containing our poem, and it is the most carefully produced; but one should be wary of a stemma that would place its text of *Amys and Amylion* significantly closer to the hypothetical original redaction than Douce.

2. Main literary differences between the English texts

The differences between the extant texts of *Amys and Aymlion* are minor but interesting. Some appear to derive from the scribes' awareness of the various literary traditions of their subject-matter. All the manuscripts refer to the work as a *geste*, but S also calls the poem a *romance*;[33] similarly, all manuscripts state that Amylion's faithful servant is named Oweys, but A also provides his nickname Amoraunt, as in the Anglo-Norman romance. On the other hand, the heroine is consistently called Belesawnt, as in the *chanson de geste*, with no mention of either the name (Mirabele) or the nickname (Florie) given to her in the Anglo-Norman romance. Most discrepancies however reflect the scribes' different readings of the poem they were copying.

The main area of variation, as may be expected, is in the depiction of feminine characters. The misogynistic tendency present in all versions of the tale, though mitigated to some extent in the English romance, still gives rise to revealing reworkings on the part of the individual scribes. D thus stands apart from the other texts by deleting all mention of the heroes' mothers as sources of parental authority (see especially 11:2); this is an all-male world in

---

[32] The dubious nature of certain presuppositions is demonstrated in connection with the French texts by BAR.

[33] S refers to the work as a *geste* once only, 34:1, where the word is at the rhyme and could not therefore easily be changed. The term romance appears to have corresponded better to the scribe's perception of the poem he was copying.

which women are merely tolerated. The absence of the mother-figures when Amys and Amylion are handed over to their new surrogate parent, the duke, puts into perspective the absence of Belesawnt when her children are murdered by their father, and her apparently heartless reaction to the news of their death. Even Belesawnt's mother can do nothing for her child beyond acting as pledge for Amys, and it is certainly no mere chance that the seduction is indirectly due to her, since she is the one who coaxes Belesawnt into the garden where she will meet Amys. Mothers do not know best in this world, and when they are present they cause more mischief than anything else.[34] This masculinist outlook is also found in the account of Belesawnt's deflowering, which D and A view as an achievement of the hero (*he wan here maidenhede*, 62:11), while H describes it as the heroine's loss (*she lostyn here maydynhede*). As may be expected, this bias also colours the way the spouses are shown relating to each other. Amylion's wife, seeing the naked sword placed in her bed between her and her supposed husband, thus looks *wrothly* at him in A and S, but *wordely*, which may arguably be glossed as "in a worthy manner", in D;[35] and her subsequent rejection of her husband announced by the angel is extended to *her* kin (D, 104:10) rather than *his* (S), thus implicitly reintroducing the epic "evil blood" theme present in the *chanson de geste*. Similarly, Belesawnt's reaction when she is told of her children's death is exceedingly cold and rational in D, whereas in A we are shown a woman in empathy with the suffering of her husband: she calls him *O lef liif*, as against the more formal *sire* of D (192:4), while S has her say *have we no care*, which associates her with Amys's distress more directly than D's *have thou no care* (192:6).

Another area where variant readings have some impact on the overall image given by the work is what may be termed the rationalising, even realistic strain we find more especially in A. Amys's attempt to dissuade Belesawnt from becoming his lover is expanded into an additional stanza in the manuscript, possibly to justify the heroine's petulant reaction; but as a result, Amys's responsibility is minimized. Another instance may be found in the depiction of the life as beggars of Aymlion and Oweys, which in A covers two stanzas unrepresented in the other texts: the first one (see note 138-139) describes the prosperity of the land and Amoraunt's happiness, while the second (see note 148-149) recounts Amoraunt's hardships when he has to carry his lord, and the indignity of their both falling in the mud. This puts a greater emphasis on the otherwise shadowy character of Amoraunt/Oweys, but more importantly

---

[34] The only exception to this rule is the Virgin Mary; S gives her special importance by stating that the miracle of the resurrection of Amys's children happens *Through the beseching of his* [i.e., Christ's] *mother dere*.

[35] However, considering the tendency for our scribe to use $d/t/t h$ interchangeably, and the generally misogynistic colouring of the D-text, it is more probable that we just have here a variant of *wrothly*.

underlines the utter helplessness of Amylion, who in the other English texts retains more dignity. Indeed, the scribe of A is so heavy-handed that the whole scene becomes suspiciously close to comparable scenes in fabliaux, which are meant to be comic rather than melodramatic. In another stanza peculiar to A, Amys demands to know how the beggar got the cup before starting to beat him: a more rational behaviour than that shown in the other texts, but which undermines the parallel between the duke Amys and his former lord, the duke whose daughter he had seduced. And finally, Amys's decision to kill his children is given additional justification by the insertion of a stanza where we are told that the angel tells him to do so three nights running: a detail which exonerates him from the full responsibility for the horror of his act, but also increases the disparity between the two friends, since Amys needs a triple vision to bring himself to do his duty towards Amylion.

By contrast, D tends to delete passages which appear to have no narrative function beyond adding verisimilitude to the situation. The duke's words to Amylion when he leaves court to get married (19:7-12) are what would be expected on such an occasion, but they play no role in the plot: they disappear from D, even though they are present in all the other extant manuscripts. The same principle of narrative economy appears to be at the root of the compression of stanza 36, where the last three lines describing Amys's prowess are missing from D, possibly because those three lines are repeated almost verbatim in stanza 37. The statement that the leper Amylion was banned from his hall and from the high table (128:6-8) may similarly have been deleted in D because of its apparent contradiction with the immediate context.[36]

On the whole, however, all the extant manuscripts have handed down to us a poem that is recognisably the same; the areas of agreement are such that it would be excessive to talk of different versions, rather than different texts, of *Amys and Amylion*.

3. Editions

To date, the poem has been edited three times in its entirety: in 1810 by Henry Weber; in 1884 by Eugen Kölbing; and in 1937 by MacEdward Leach. Weber's edition is based on A, with the missing beginning and end supplied from D, and a single reference to H. S was not known to him.[37] Kölbing's edition was the first to be based on all the manuscripts; his study includes editions of other versions of the story: the Anglo-Norman romance, the Latin *Vita Amici et Amelii carissimorum*, and the Icelandic *Amicus ok Amelius Rimur*. Moreover,

---

[36] The following stanza tells us that the leper stayed in his hall for six months. This problem does not occur in A, where for *out of his halle*, we read *in his owhen halle*.

[37] The poem in WEBER is to be found in vol. 2, pp.367-474.

19

Kölbing's introduction provides the reader with a detailed analysis of the phonology, stylistics and sources of the poem. The base manuscript of Kölbing's edition is A, with variant readings from SDH indicated in his apparatus; a composite text completes the passages missing in A. The third scholarly edition of *Amys and Amylion*, by MacEdward Leach for the Early English Text Society, is now the standard reference for the poem. The philological and stylistic part of his introduction is not as painstakingly detailed as Kölbing's, but Leach provides a useful outline of the possible sources and the development of the story in European literature. His edition, like Kölbing's, is based on A, supplemented in its missing parts by what Leach considered the best variant reading — in practice, that of S, with occasional readings from D.

The present edition is based on one manuscript only, MS Douce 326. This choice was dictated by two considerations. First, this is the only extant manuscript to preserve a complete version of *Amys and Amylion*: its coherent text means that it is not necessary to interpolate extensive sections from other manuscripts in order to produce a readable poem. But more importantly, this one-manuscript edition remedies to some extent the neglect which this redaction of the poem has suffered, by making available an interesting witness that has up to now mostly been reduced to variant readings in a critical apparatus.

As noted above, the Douce text of *Amys and Amylion* is shorter than that of A, due to the absence of a number of isolated lines and full stanzas found in A. It must be stressed that these "missing" lines and stanzas in no way detract from the coherence of the Douce version. Indeed, in most cases, their extremely conventional nature and repetitive contents make one suspect that some of them at least are scribal "improvements"; none of the 6 stanzas in the Auchinleck text not found in Douce are represented in H and S. These stanzas are therefore here reduced to footnotes, with the same "modernized" spelling principles as those adopted for our main text. Isolated "missing" lines have been inserted in the text, between square brackets, in order to preserve the twelve-line stanza pattern throughout the poem. This was perhaps not absolutely necessary, since Middle English romances frequently have stanzas of six or nine lines; but the presence of these lines in manuscripts other than just Auchinleck on a few occasions suggested that, for the sake of consistency, all stanzas in Douce ought to be "completed". In so doing, preference has been given to the readings of S, which is more closely related to Douce than Auchinleck; spelling has been aligned on that of D.

The principle on which this edition is founded is one of conservatism tempered by the demands of clarity. Word division, capitalisation and punctuation are modern; *u*/*v* have been redistributed according to vocalic or consonant function, while thorn and yogh, which occur only rarely in our text, are transcribed as *th* and *gh* or *y*.[38] Abbreviations are silently expanded, with the exception of smaller figures in roman numerals, which have been retained. In all other respects, however, the edition aims at reproducing the manuscript text as faithfully as possible. Emendation is introduced only to correct obvious errors; if sense can be extracted from a line, it is left to stand, and discussed in a footnote. The apparatus only indicates instances where the printed text does not follow MS Douce. However, for the reader who wishes to have an idea of the main divergences of characterisation or plot between the manuscripts of *Amys and Amylion*, the footnotes record major variants which change the colouring of a passage or betray a slight difference in the narrator's stance.

Emendations may be put under two headings:
(a) minor scribal errors
(b) corrupt words or lines.
The majority of the emendations come under (a). They may all be explained by a simple *lapsus calami* or by a faulty deciphering of either a letter or an abbreviation at some point of the transmission of the text:[39]

3:5 ladyes *free* to-fonde (= H,S) - D ladyes for tofonde; 4:1 *as* thei h. (=H) - D a thei h.; 8:11 *Ne* knew (= S) - D That knew; 9:9 for to *kithe* (= A,H,S) - D for to kepe; 21:7 with *drery* mode (= A,H) - D with rery mode; 23:3 redy to *boun* (= A) - D redy to hem; 23:4 with an *hurt* herde - D with an hend herde; 39:1 When *thei* (= A,S,H) - D When sche; 44:10 here *hert* (= A,S) - D here; 44:12 *no* glee (= A,H) - D - ne glee; 46:9 with *him* (= A,H) - D with here; 56:5 as *princes* (= A,H) - D As princers; 56:6 *mariness* - D marners; 57:7 And *be* here s. (= A,S,H) - D And he here s.; 62:12 Ere than *she* went (= S,H) - D Ere than he went; 70:6 *Avowed* (= S,H) - D Aswonde; 70:12 And *sen* (= A,S,H) - D And seth; 74:3 all that *ther* were (= A,S,H) - D all that the were; 74:4 nyght *and* day (= A,S) - D night day; 90:10 spede (= A,S) - D spde; 103:1 And as *he* rode (= A,S) - D And as rode; 107:9 Thei *scheverede* (= S) - D Thei schonerede; 113:10 And after *lad* (= A,S) - D And after had; 114:7 The *Ffor* at the beginning of the following line was erroneously anticipated by the scribe; 117:11 He told (= A,S) - D To tell; 126:9 *everichon* (= A,S) - D everchon; 158:2 e*very*chone (= A) - D evychone; 165:1 The *duke* ansuerd (= A) - D The ansuerd; 175:10 *bedde* (= A) - D bathe; 183:2 To *the* chamber (= A,S) - D To

---

[38] Thorn occurs almost exclusively in abbreviations for *the* (5 cases), *that* (84 cases), *thei* (2 cases), *then* (1 case), *ther* (1 case) or *thou* (12 cases). Otherwise, thorn only appears once in our manuscript, in the word *blythe* (14:4). Moreover, the erroneous reading in 9:9 (MS *to kepe*) appears to be due to a faulty decoding of thorn as *p*. Yogh transcribed as *y* appears 9 times in the adverb *yare* and once in the verb *yode* (139:6); transcribed as *g* it occurs once, in *agayn* (144:4); transcribed as *gh*, it occurs twice in *thaugh* (127:9 and 136:8) and once in the verb *taught* (118:8). Moreover, the *z* in the word *lazar/lazur* is identical in shape to yogh.

[39] The spelling variations of the different manuscripts are not recorded.

his chamber; 184:5 Ffor *me* he sched (= S) - D Ffor he sched; 191:8 *An* aungell (= A,S) - D And aungell; 194:10 thei *wept* (= S) - D thei went; 201:9 *The* hende knyghtes (= S) - D That hende knyghtes.

Some of these relatively straightforward emendations require justification: 23:3 redy to *boun* - D redy to hem. The reading of A was chosen here against that of H (*gon*) because *boun* is visually closer to *him*, and preserves the rhyme scheme of the stanza.

23:4 With an *hurt* herde to hide - D With an hend herde to hide. This emendation preserves the alliterative pattern of the line whilst restoring sense; however, it is supported by none of the other manuscripts. Cp. *Hende, herkeneth! Is nought to hide* (A) or *Bothe the knyghts fayre of hyde* (H).

56:6 With merthes and *mariness* - D With merthes and marners. A miscounting of minims added to a confusion between the long *s* and *r* best accounts for D's *marners*. The other manuscripts are of little help here: *With menske and mirthe* (A), *With worschup and mirthe* (H) and *With metes and drynkese* (S).

The emendations under (b) are more complex. There are 7 in all, of varying importance:

33:5 to *schende* (= A,H,S) - D to se. Both the meaning of the stanza and the testimony of the other manuscripts suggest *schende* is the correct reading here.

33:8 With wreth and wyn and loreand chere - D With wreth and wynd lordand fere. *wynd* is probably due to the anticipation of *and* after *wyn*; *lordand* is certainly a misreading of *loreand* (= A, and *louryng*, H). *fere* may be a rationalisation on the scribe's part, who appears to have understood *wynd lordand fere* as Noun + Gerund + Adverb.

160:2 *What* foly, *he seyd*, gan *he* sayn - D With foly cause gan sayn - cp. A: *What foly, he seyd, can he sain.* An obviously corrupt line. The reading *with* for *what* is easily explained; the disappearance of *he seyd* may be due to the anticipation of *can he*, misread as *cause*. *gan* would then have been added to give the resulting line an acceptable syntactical structure.

173:12 Ffor Him that this worlde gan - D Ffor Him this worldle gan. Cp. *Ffor him that this world wan* (A). Even though *gan* has not been emended, it is probably a misreading of *wan*, with an initial wynn. The scribe presumably understood it as a substantive rather than a verb, hence the deletion of *that* and the transformation of the substantive *worlde* into the adjective *worldle*.

178:5 The *hert* blode (= A) - D And with the blode. Cp. S: *The blod.* The reading of D is not acceptable for syntactical reasons; that of S is metrically incomplete. I have therefore adopted the conventional phrase found in A.

198:7-8 And all that thei ther *raughte* (S: *araught*) / Grete strokes there thei *caughte* (= S)- D And all that thei ther laste / Grete strokes there thei causte. The *-ste* endings of the two verbs may be explained by a scribal misreading of

22

yogh as s. Since *laughte* does not make sense in the context, it has been emended to *raughte*, the verb suggested by S.

One may note that for a fifteenth-century copy by an allegedly careless scribe, the number of serious emendations required by the text is remarkably low.

D. Select Bibliography

I. Sources

Editions of the English text:

Eugen KÖLBING, *Amis and Amiloun*, Heilbronn: Henninger, 1884
MacEdward LEACH, *Amis and Amiloun*, London: Oxford University Press, 1937 (Early English Text Society, no.203)
Henry WEBER, *Metrical Romances of the Thirteenth, Fourteenth and Fifteenth Centuries*, Edinburgh: George Ramsay, 1810

Editions of the Latin and French texts:

Peter F. DEMBOWSKI ed., *Ami et Amile, chanson de geste*, Paris: Champion, 1969 (Classiques français du moyen âge 97)
Hideka FUKUI, *Amys e Amillyoun*, London: Anglo-Norman Text Society, 1990 (Plain texts series 7)
Eugen KÖLBING ed., *Amis and Amiloun*, Heilbronn: Henninger, 1884; *Vita Amici et Amelii*: pp.xcvii-cx; Anglo-Norman romance: pp.111-187
Marbury B. OGLE and Dorothy M. SCHULLIAN eds., *Rodulfi Tortarii Carmina*, American Academy in Rome: Rome, 1933 (Papers and Monographs of the American Academy in Rome viii)

II. Dictionaries

J. BOSWORTH and T.N. TOLLER, *An Anglo-Saxon Dictionary* (1882-98); Supplement by T.N. TOLLER (1891). Revised ed., London, 1972
H. KURATH and S.M. KUHN, *Middle English Dictionary*, London: Oxford University Press, 1956-
F.M. STRATMAN, *A Middle English Dictionary*; Revised by H. BRADLEY, London: Clarendon Press, 1891
W. VON WARTBURG, *Französisches Etymologisches Wörterbuch: eine Darstellung des galloromanisches Sprachschatzes*, Bonn, then Basel, 1928—

III. Studies

A. On the English poem

Dean R. BALDWIN, "*Amis and Amiloun*: The Testing of Treuthe", *Papers on Language and Literature* 16 (1980): 353-65
Susan DANNENBAUM, "Insular Tradition in the Story of *Amis and Amiloun*", *Neophilologus* 67 (1983): 611-22
Kathryn HUME, "*Amis and Amiloun* and the Aesthetics of Middle English Romance", *Studies in Philology* 70 (1973): 19-41

Eugen KÖLBING, "Vier Romanzen-Handschriften", *Englische Studien* 7 (1884): 177-91

Dale KRAMER, "Structural Artistry in *Amis and Amiloun*", *Annuale Mediaevale* 9 (1968): 103-122

Ojar KRATINS, "The Middle English *Amis and Amiloun*: Chivalric Romance or Secular Hagiography?", *PMLA* 81 (1966): 347-54

B. On the Latin and French texts

Francis BAR, —Raoul le Tourtier et la chanson de geste d'*Ami et Amile*", in *La chanson de geste et le mythe carolingien (Mélanges René Louis publiés par ses collègues, ses amis et ses élèves à l'occasion de son 75e anniversaire)*, Saint-Père-sous-Vézelay, 1982, II, 973-86

Gédéon HUET, "*Ami et Amile*. Les origines de la légende", *Le Moyen Age* 31 (1919): 162-86

Kathryn HUME, "Structure and Perspective. Romance and Hagiographic Features in the Amicus and Amelius Story", *Journal for English and Germanic Philology* 69 (1970), 89-107

A.H. KRAPPE, "The Legend of Amicus and Amelius", *The Modern Language Review* 18 (1929): 152-61

Huguette LEGROS, "Quand les jugements de Dieu deviennent artifices littéraires ou la profanité impunie d'une poétique", in *La Justice au moyen âge (Sanction ou impunité?)*, Aix-en-Provence: Université de Provence, 1986 (Senefiance 16), 197-212.

Geneviève MADIKA, "La religion dans *Ami et Amile*", in *Ami et Amile (Une chanson de geste de l'amitié)*, ed. Jean DUFOURNET, Paris: Champion, 1987 (Unichamp 16), 39-50

Max MANITIUS, *Geschichte der lateinischen Literatur des Mittelalters*, Munich: C.H. Beck, 1931, vol 3, 872-77

Philippe MENARD, "La légende d'*Ami et Amile* au XIIe siècle: la chanson de geste et les traditions antérieures", in *Bien dire et bien aprandre*, special issue "Sur *Ami et Amile*", 1988, 7-13

Emanuel MICKEL, "The Question of Guilt in *Ami et Amile*", *Romania* 106 (1985): 19-35

Geneviève PICHON, "La Lèpre dans *Ami et Amile*", in *Ami et Amile (Une chanson de geste de l'amitié)*, ed. Jean DUFOURNET, Paris: Champion, 1987 (Unichamp 16), 51-68

Alice PLANCHE, "*Ami et Amile* ou le Même et l'Autre", in *Zeitschrift für romanische Philologie*, Sonderband zum 100jährigen Bestehen (1977): 237-69

F.J.E. RABY, *A History of Secular Latin Poetry in the Middle Ages*, Oxford: Clarendon, 1934, vol.2, 23-26

Samuel N. ROSENBERG, "Lire *Ami et Amile*, le regard sur les personnages féminins", in *Ami et Amile (Une chanson de geste de l'amitié)*, éd. Jean DUFOURNET, Paris: Champion, 1987 (Unichamp 16), 69-78

Thomas E. VESCE, "Reflections on the Epic Quality of *Ami et Amiles*", *Mediaeval Studies* 35 (1973), 129-45

C. General

Saul Nathaniel BRODY, *The Disease of the Soul. Leprosy in Medieval Literature*, Ithaca and London: Cornell University Press, 1974

Urs DÜRMÜLLER, *Narrative Possibilities of the Tail-Rime Romance*, Bern: Francke Verlag, 1975 (Swiss Studies in English, 83)

Vladimir Ja. PROPP, *Morphologie du Conte, suivi de Les Transformations des contes merveilleux*, trad. Marguerite DERRIDA, Tzvetan TODOROV and Claude KAHN, Paris: Seuil, 1973

P. REMY, "La Lèpre, thème littéraire au moyen âge", *Le Moyen Age* 52 (1946): 195-242

Susan WITTIG, *Stylistic and narrative structures in the Middle English romances*, Austin and London: University of Texas Press, 1978

Hic incipit vita de Amys et Amylion.

1   FFOR Goddis love in trinyte
Alle that ben hende herkneth to me,
Y pray you paramour,
What whilom fille beyonde the see
Off twoo barons of grete bounte,
And men of grete honour.
Her faders were barons hende,
Lordyngs semyng of grete kende,
Price in town and toure.
To here of the childeryn twoo,
How thei were in wele and woo,
Ywys, yt is grete douloure!

2   In wele and woo how thei gone wende,
And howe unknow thei were of kende,
The berdes bolde of chere;
And how thei were guode and hende,
And how yong thei become frende,
In courte where as thei were;
And how thei were dobbid knyght,
And how thei were trewth plyght,
The childerin both in ffere;
And in whate cuntre thei were born,

1:4 This line, which depends on *herkneth to me* (1.2), introduces the subject-matter of the poem: "Listen to me [telling you about] what happened in the past...".

1:8 For the line to make sense, *semyng* must be understood as "seemly" rather than "seeming": "Noble lords of high birth".

1:9 "Prize in town and tower": i.e. the best you can find. The tower refers here to the castle of the lord of the town; the expression thus denotes society's unanimity in valuing the heroes' fathers.

2:2 "And how they came from unrelated families". This reading emphasizes the wondrous nature of the resemblance between the two heroes, since it excludes any rationalising through hypothetical blood-links. The line has also been understood as meaning: "And how extraordinary they were in character", or "Of what unknown ancestry they were" (see Leach, p.113).

2:6 *where as* is a compound conjunction, "where".

And whate the childern names weren:
Herkenyth, and ye may here.

3   In Lombardye, y understonde,
Whilom befille in that londe,
In geste as we rede,
Off twoo barons hende of honde
And hadde twoo ladyes *free* to-fonde
That worthi were in wede.
Uppon thes hende ladies twoo
Twoo knave childern were goten thoo
That dowthi were of dede
And trewe were in alle thing:
Therfore Jhesu heven king
Ffull wele quited here mede.

4   The childern names, *as* thei hight
In ryme y wille you rede ryght
And telle in my talkyng;
Bothe were goten on o nyght
And on o day yborn aplyght,
Fforsoth withoute lesyng.
Thet oon barons sone, ywysse,
He was callid syre Amys
At the chirche at his crystenyng.
Thet other was callid syre Amylion;
He was a childe of grete renoun,
Ycomen of hye ospryng.

3:5 *l. free to f.* - MS *l. for to f.*; 4:1 *as thei h.* - MS *a thei h.*

3:3 The source of the poem is consistently called a *geste*, not (as one may have expected) a romance; elsewhere (37:3), it is referred to as a *boke*, but also as *talkyng* (40:4).

3:5 *free to-fonde*: previous editors have understood *to fonde* as the infinitive of *fonde*, meaning "try", "tempt", "prove"; however, it is more likely that we have the past participle of the verb "find", with the prefix *to-*. The use of the prefix *to-* where one would have expected the prefix *be-* is quite common in later Middle English texts. The meaning in both cases is roughly identical: "most noble".

3:12: "Gave them a very good reward"; literally: "Very well repaid their reward".

5   The childerin gon thoo thryve
And fayrer were there non alyve,
Both curteys, hende and guode.
When thei were of yeres fyve,
All here kynne was of hem blyth,
So mylde thei were of mode.
When thei were vii yere olde, ywys,
Every man hadde of hem blysse
To behalde that erthly fode.
When thei were xii yere olde,
In all that londe was ther non to beholde
So ffayre of bone and blode.

6   In that tyme, as y understonde,
A douty duke woned in that londe,
Pryse in town and toure,
Ffor he lette sende his sonde
After barons, free and bonde,
And ladyes bryght in boure;
A ryche feste he wolde make
And alle for Jhesu Crystes sake
That ys oure Savyour.
Moche folk, as y you say,
He lette sende theder that day
With myrth and grete honour.

7   The two barons that y of tolde
And here sonnes faire and bolde,
To courte thei come full yare.
Whan thei served yong and olde,
Many men gan hem beholde,
Off lordyngs that there ware,
Howe thei were of body bryght

5:9 *erthly fode: fode*, though singular in form, is plural in meaning; *erthly* may be corrupt; the other manuscripts read *frely fode*, "noble children". As it stands the expression may be understood as: "These living [i.e. in and of this world] children".

7:4 *Thei* refers to the heroes. Our manuscript is the only one to suggest that the two boys helped at the serving of the meal, thus foreshadowing their future functions at the duke's court.

7:5-6: "Many men among the lords who were there observed them".

Off hide, hewe and here.
Alle thei saide withoute les,
Ffairer childer than thes wes
Ne saw thei never ere.

8   In alle the courte was ther no wyght,   [14b]
Erle, baron, squyer no knyght,
Nether love no lothe —
So like thei were both of syght
And of on wexing ryght —
In sawe y say forsothe,
In all thing thei were lyche —
Ther was nother power ne ryche
Who that beheld hem both
Ffayrer never more ne cowde say,
Ne knew thet oon of the childern tway,
Bote be colowr of here cloth.

9   The ryche duke his feste gan holde
Off erls and barouns bolde,
As ye may leste and lythe,
Ffourthenyghte, as men tolde,
With mete and drynke and myrth on molde.
To glade the barouns blythe
There was game and melodie
Off all maner menstralsye,
Here craftes for to *kithe*,

8:11 *Ne knew t.o.* - MS *That k.* ; 9:9 *to kithe* - MS *to kepe*

8:3 "Neither favourably or badly disposed", i.e. everyone without
exception. Line 8 ("neither poor nor rich") has the same connotation of "no
one at all". The syntax of this stanza is somewhat complicated. The subject
("nobody") is separated from the rest of the main clause ("could say which
was the fairer, or tell one child from the other"), by a parenthetical comment
of the narrator (ll.6-7) on the two preceding lines. The broken thread is picked
up again on l.8, where the subject is repeated.

8:10 Other MSS read here: *Fader ne moder that couth say*; this further
emphasizes the resemblance of the boys. On the absence of the heroes'
mothers in our text, see Introduction, pp.17-18.

9:9 The manuscript reading (*to kepe*) has been emended to make it conform
to the rhyme scheme, and improve the sense. The emended text, which
follows the reading of the other MSS, may be translated as follows (ll.6-9):

Tyll the xv day full yare
Thei toke leve and wolde fare
And thanked him many sythe.

10   When all the lordings schulde wende
The riche duke, comely of kende,
To him he clepid that tyde
The trewe barouns guode and hende
And besought them, as thei were frende,
In courte with him to abide
And lete here sonnes that were free
In service with him for to be,
Semely to go be his syde:
"And y schall make hem knyghtes twoo
And find hem well for ever moo
As lordings prowd in prede."

11   Tho twoo barons aunsuerd agayn
And with here mouthes thei gan sayn
To the duke full yare
That thei were both glad and fayn
That here leve sonnes twayn
In servyse with him were;
Thei yave here childerin here blyssing
And besought Jhesu heven kyng
Ffor to childe hem fro kare.
Ofte thei thanked the duke that dai;
Thei toke leve and went here wai
And to here cuntrey thei fare.

"To please the merry lords there was entertainment and music from all sorts of minstrels exhibiting their skills".

10:5 *as thei were frende*, "as true as they were friends", i.e. "in the name of their friendship".

10:12 *prowd in prede*: despite the pejorative connotations of the modern reflexes of the words in this expression, it is here entirely positive. Like *free to-fonde* (3:5) it indicates nobility, and may be glossed as "splendid in honour".

11:2 *here*: "their". Our text has both *h-* and *th-* forms for the third person plural of the personal pronoun; see Glossary, **he**. For *mouthes*, MS H reads *moderys*, MS A *leuedis* and MS S *ladies*.

12   Thus the leve childerin, ywys,
Childe Amylion and childe Amys,
In court thei were in fere
To ryde an huntyng under the rys;
Of all that londe thei bare the prys
And worthiest were in wede.
So well the childerin loved thoo
Were never childerin that loved soo,
Nether in worde ne in dede;
Ne betuene men of flesche and bone
Trewer love was never none,
In jeste ryght as we rede.

13   On a dai, the childerin ware and wight
Togeder were trouth plight
While thei leved in londe:
Bote be dai and be nyght,
In wele, wo, wrong and ryght
Fferly scholde hem fonde,
Hold togeder at every nede,
In wele, woo, word and dede,
While thei myght stonde,
Ffro that dai forward ever moo,
Nether faile other for wele ne woo:
Therto thei halde up honde.

14   Thus, in jeste as ye mowe here,
The hende childerin in court were
With the duke for to abide.
The duke was blythe and glad of chere;
Thei were him both lefe and dere,
Semely to gon by side.
Whenne thei were xvi yere olde,
He dubbed hem barones bolde,
Knyghtes in that tyde,

13:4-11 We have here the contents, in reported speech, of the oath of the heroes: "Both by day and by night, in prosperity, sadness, wrong and right, they would fairly support each other and hold together whenever necessary; in good fortune and adversity, in word and in deed, for as long as they could stand, from that day onwards and for ever, neither should fail the other, in good fortune or in adversity". The repetitions in the passage underline the solemnity of the oath.

And fond hem all that was nede:
Hors and wepen and wordely wede,
As lordings proude in prede.

15   So well the duke loved hem thoo,
        All that thei wold, he fonde hem soo,
        Stedes white and broune.
        To what stede that thei gon goo,   [15a]
        Alle that lond spake of hem twoo,
        Both in towre and town;
        Into whate sted that thei went,
        At justes or at tornement,
        Sire Amys and sire Amylion —
        Ffor doughtyest thei were in dede,
        With spere and schelde to ryde on stede —
        Thei gate hem grete renown.

16   The ryche duke tolde of hem grete prys,
        For thei were both ware and wys,
        And men of grete bounte.
        Syre Amylion and sire Amys,
        He toke hem both in grete affys,
        In his court for to be.
        Sire Amys, as ye mow here,
        He made him his chief botelere,
        [Ffor he was hend and fre];
        Syre Amylion, over hem all,
        He made him steward in his hall
        To dight all his mayne.

16:9 Supplied from S - om. MS

14:11 *wordely wede*, "expensive clothes". This is a good example of our
scribe's use of *d/t/th* interchangeably.

16:1 "the noble duke held them in great esteem"; or: "said a lot of good of
them".

16:8 *Chief botelere*: an important office. The chief butler was responsible
for the supplies of food and drink at the court.

16:11 "steward in his hall": the steward in hall was a sort of master of
ceremonies, responsible for the seating of guests at table, and whose duty it
was to keep order in the court; hence l.12: "to rule his entire household".

17   Than hadde the duke, y understond,
A chefe steward of all his lond,
A doughty knyght at crye.
Ever he preved with ye and hond
To bring the childerin into schond,
With gyle and trecherye:
For thei were both guode and hend,
And so well the duke here frend,
He hadde therof enemy.
To the duke, with wordes grame,
Ever he preved to do hem schame,
With grete felonye.

18   And so, withinne yeres twoo,
To syre Amylyon ther come thoo
A messanger hende in hond,
And saide that God had taken him fro
His fader, and his moder also,
Thoroght grace of His sonde.
Thoo was the knyght a carfull man,
And to the duke he seide than,
And dide him to understonde,

16-17 MS A has an extra stanza at this point, on the universal love and praise that the heroes won in the discharging of their duties (Leach, 193-204): *In to her seruise when thai were brought, / To geten hem los tham spared nought, / Wel hendeliche thai bigan; / With riche & pouer so wele thai wrought /Al that hem seiye with word and thought, / Hem loued mani a man; / For thai were so blithe of chere, / Ouer al the lond fer and nere / The los of loue thai wan, / & the riche douke, withouten les, / Of alle the men that olive wes, Mest he loued hem than.*

17:2 *chefe steward*: officer in charge of the general expenditure and book-keeping.

17:3 *at crye*: a French expression meaning literally "at call", i.e. subject to the vassalic duty of answering the overlord's summons.

17:4 *With ye and hond*: the other MSS have here the more pejorative *with nith/speche/envy and ond*, "with malice/speech/envy and hatred".

17:9 *He hadde enemy*: one would have expected here *envy* (the reading of the other MSS) instead of *enemy*. However, *enemy* is attested in Kurath and Kuhn as meaning "hostility", and is metrically satisfying; I have therefore let it stand.

18:3 *hende in hond*: literally, "gracious in hand", i.e. in deeds. A conventional phrase denoting nobility.

His fader and his moder hend
Were dede and he most wend
Ffor to receyve his lond.

19 The ryche duke comely of kynde
Answerd him with wordes hende
And saide: "So God me spede,
Syre Amylion, thou schalt wend.
Y was never so wo for frend
That oute of my cuntrey yede!
[But yf it ever befal soo
That thow falle in werre or woo,
That thou have to me nede,
Savely com and send thy sond:
With al the power of my londe
I wreke the of thy dede.]"

20 Then was Amylion ferly woo;
Ffro his brother for to goo
Ever him was all his thought.
To a goldsmyth he went thoo,
And lete werke golde cuppys twoo
That for three hundred pound were bought.
Both thei were of on wyght
And of on mykyll, y plyght;
So quentelye thei were wrought,
In all thing were thei like, ywis,
As Amylion and sire Amys,
That thei laked ryght noght.

19:7-12 Supplied from S - om. MS ; 20:6 *three hundred pound* - MS *iii C lb*

19:3: *So God me spede*, "May God assist me". *So/As* + Subject (God/Christ/Mary) + Object (*me*) + Verb (in subj.) is a standard formula for oaths, and is commonly used to give emphasis to greetings, promises, statements, etc. It is found throughout the poem.
19:7-12 This promise of the duke is presented here as an indication of his great love for Amylion; but it is also the conventional expression of a lord's duty of assistance towards his vassal. The promise, however, is never put to use in the rest of the poem.
20:12 "they had absolutely nothing lacking" – i.e. they were absolutely identical.

21   When sire Amylion was yare,
He toke his leve for to fare
To wend in his jurne.
Syre Amys, for thought and kare,
For mornyng and sekyng sare,
Allmost swonned that free;
And to the duke with *drery* mode
He besought him there he stode:
"Syre, par charyte,
Yef me leve to fare the froo.
Bote yefe y mai with my brother goo,
My herte wyll breke at three."

22   The ryche duke comely of kende
Answerd with wordes hende
Withoute more delay:
"Syre Amys, my leve frende,
Wold ye bothe fro me wende?
Certes," he saide, "nay.
Yefe ye were both went me froo,
Then were come all my woo:
My joye were away.
Thi brother schall home to his cuntre;
With him wend in his jurne,
And come ayen this day."

23   When thei were redy to ryde,
The doughty knyghtes that tyde,
Ther hors come redy to *boun*.

21:7 *w. drery m.* - MS *w. rery m.*; 23:3 *redy to boun* - MS *redy to hem*

22:7-9 *were* is here a subjunctive, expressing our conditional: "If you both went away from me, then my sorrow would be complete, my joy would be gone".

22:11-12 The contradiction in these two lines is only apparent: the *jurne* must be understood as the amount of travelling made in one day, rather than the journey in the modern sense of the word.

23:3-4 Our MS is corrupt at this point, but the general meaning is clear: [When the knights were ready] "their horses were brought to them ready to set off, and hiding their pain with difficulty", [they went away].

36

With an *hurt* herde to hide,
Thei bosked hem in that tyde
And went oute of the town;   [15b]
And all wey as thei rade,
Grete mornyng the knyghtes made,
Syre Amys and Amylion,
Tyll that thei schulde parte atwayn.
Well fayre uppon a playn,
Off hors thei light adoun.

24   And when thei were afote ylyght,
Syre Amylion that gentill knyght,
Well wyse he was of rede.
To sire Amys he said anone ryght:
"Brother, we are trowth-plyght,
Both in word and dede.
Ffro this dai forward ever moo,
Nother faile other, for well ne woo,
To helpe other at nede.
Brother, be now trew to me,
And y schall be as trew to the,
As wys God me spede!"

25   "Of o thing, brother, y warn the beforn:
Ffor Gods love that bare the croun of thorn
To save all mankynde,
Be notte ayen thi lord forsworn.
Yef thou do thou arte forlorn,
Ever withouten ende.
Be ever trew withoute treson,
And thenk on me sire Amylion.
Now we atwo schull wende;
But o thing, brother, y forbede the:
Ffro the fals steward rede the,
Ffor certes he will the schend."

23:4 *w. an hurt h.* - MS *w. an hend h.*

24:12 "As truly as the wise God will protect me", or "May the wise God
protect me": See note 19:3 above.

26   And as thei stode, the barons bold,
Sire Amylion toke ii couppes of gold
That were like in all thing,
And bad sire Amys that he schuld
Chose whather that he wolde
Withoute more duellyng,
And seid to him: "My leve brother,
Kepe thou that on, and y that other.
Ffor Jhesu heven king,
Lette never this couppe fro the,
But loke heron and thenk on me,
In tokne of oure parting."

27   Grete sorow thei made at here parting,
And keste togeder without lesing,
The knyghtes hend and free,
And betaugh hem to Jhesu heven king;
And on here stedes thei gon spring,
And went in here jurne.
Sire Amylion went into his lond
And all he seised into his hond,
And his faders had he;
And after spoused a lady bryght in boure
And brought here home with grete honour
And grete solempnite.

28   Lete we now sire Amylion be
With his lady in his cuntre —
God yeve him well to fare! —
And of sire Amys lestneth to me.
When he come to court aye,
How blyth of him thei were!
Ffor he was ever trew and guode,
All him blessed, bone and blode,
All that him gate and bare,

26:3 "That were similar in every respect".
27:9 "He had his father's property".
27:10 "bright in bower": a conventional alliterating phrase denoting feminine beauty. The same phrase is later used of the duke's daughter and her maidens.
28:9 "All who looked upon him and mixed with him". This is in apposition to the "all" in l.8.

Save the steward of the londe.
Ever he preved with ye and hond
To bring him into kare.

29   And on a dai yt befill soo,
With the steward he mette thoo,
And he hailed that free,
And seide: "Sire Amys, the ys woo
That thi brother ys went the froo;
And certes, so ys me.
Of his wending have thou no kare:
Yef thou wilt trust to my lare
And lete thi mornyng bee,
And thou wilt be to me kend,
Y schall be to the a better frend
Than ever ryght was he."

30   "Sire Amys, do be my rede,
And we schull be brotherede,
And plight oure trouthes twoo.
Be trew to me in word and dede
And y schall, so God me rede,
Be trew to the also."
Sire Amys seid: "My trouth ys plyght
To sire Amylion, that gentyl knyght,
When he went me froo;
And while that y may go and speke,
My trouth will y noght breke,
Nether for well ne woo."

31   "Ffor be the trowth that God me send,
Y have found him so kend
Sith that y him knowe;
Ffor onys y plight trouth to that hend,   [16a]
Where in lond that y wend,
Y schall be to him trewe.

28:11 *With ye and hond*, "with eye and hand": as above (17:4), the other
MSS read *with nith/myght and ond*, "with malice and hatred".

30:2 *brotherede* is usually a substantive, meaning "brotherhood" (the sense
in which it appears in MSS A and S: *swere us b.*). However, the scribes of D
and H seem to have understood the word as the past participle of a verb
formed from the sb. "brother": "We shall be made brothers".

And yef y were now forswore,
Breke my trouth and be forlore,
Sore yt wold me rewe.
Gete me frendes wher y may:
y schall never, be nyght ne day,
Chonge him for no newe."

32   The fell steward, ther he stode,
Allmost for wrath he wex wode;
And seide withoute delay
And swore be Him that dyed on rode:
"Thou traitour, thou wykked blode!
Thou wylt abye this day,
I warne the," he said than,
"Ffor y am thi strong foman,
Be nyght and be day!"
Sire Amys answerd thoo:
"Y yef therof not on sloo.
Do ryght all that thou may."

33   Thus her wreth firste agynne;
And in wrath went atwynne
Both the knyghtes twoo.
The steward wold never blynne
To *schende* the doughty knyght of kynne,
Ever he proved thoo.
Thus in court thei were in fere
With wreth and wyn *and loreand chere*
All a yere and moo.
And after, within a lytell while,

33:5 *to schende* - MS *to se*; 33:8 *with w. and wyn and loreand chere* - MS *with w. and wynd lordand fere*

32:3-9 In MS H, the response of the steward is more suggestive of hurt feelings than in the other texts. Lines 4-6 are replaced by : *Y warne the wel knight unkynde / Of me thou hast lost a frynde / Wel truly I the say* (placed after lines 6-8 of our text). Moreover, H has three additional lines at the end of the stanza, of obscure meaning, but which emphasize further the violence of Amys's rejection of him.

32:11 "I care not a berry about it" - i.e. "I couldn't care less".

33:8 "With anger and strife and sullenness"; literally, "with sullen countenance".

The steward, with treson and gyle,
Wrought him mykill woo.

34 And in that tyme, as we rede in jeste,
The ryche duke made a feste
In semely someres tyde.
With mete and drink thei were honest,
And ther was many a ryche geste.
Than, at every syde,
Moche folk were served thare,
With erles, barons, lesse and mare,
And ladies proued in prede;
More joie myght be none
Than was in that worldely wone,
With blysse in court to abyde!

35 The ryche duke, that y of tolde,
He had a doughter faire and bolde,
Certes, hend and free.
When sche was xv yere olde
In all that lond was ther non holde
So semely on to se,
Ffor gentell sche was, and avenaunt;
Here name hight Belsauaunt,
As ye mow lyght at me.
With ladyes bryght in boure,
Sche was kept with moche honour
And grete solempnite.

36 The fest leste fourthenyght.
Of barons and ladyes so bryght
And other lordings falle,
Ther was many a gentell knyght
And many servaunt wyse and wyght
To serve the berdes all;
And the botelere syre Amys,
Over all that lond he was the prys,
Trewly to tell in tale,

35:8 *Belsauaunt*: a more correct form of the name would be Belesawnt, as
in 114:7. Metre demands that the name be trisyllabic, since it bears two
stresses.

41

[And doughtyest in every dede
And worthiest in every wede,
And chose for pris in sale.]

37   When all the lordings were gon
Oute of that wordely wone,
In boke as we rede,
The mery maide asked anon
Of here maydens everychon,
And seide: "So God you spede,
Who was the fairest knyght,
And who was the semelyest of syght
And worthiest in wede,
And who was the noblest man
That was hold in that lond than,
And doughtyest in dede?"

38   The maydens ansuerd agayn
And said: "Madame, we will you sayn
The soth, be Seint Savyour!
Of erle, baron, knyght and swayn
The fayrest body — is noght to layn —
And man of most honour,
Hit ys syre Amys the botelere.
In all this lond hath he no pere,
Nether in town ne towre;
And he ys doughtyest in dede,
And worthiest in every wede,
And chosen for the floure."

39   When *thei* had that saide, yn plyght,
Belsaunt, that berd bryght,
As ye may lestne and lythe,
On sire Amys that gentil knyght   [16b]
Here herte was leyde both day and nyght,

36:10-12 Supplied from S - om. MS; 39:1 *When thei* - MS *When sche*

36:10-12 These lines, which are missing from our MS, are three conventional phrases denoting worthiness and nobility. They are repeated almost exactly a little later (stanza 38, ll.10-12).

Dorst that no man kyde.
Wher that sche sawe him ryde or goo,
Here thought here hert broke on twoo,
That sche ne spake with that blyth;
Ffor sche ne myght nyght ne day
Speke with him, that faire may,
She weped many a sythe.

40   That mery may that was so yong,
Ffor sorow and love longyng,
Be nyght ne be day,
As y fynde in my talkyng,
Ffor sche myght speke with him nothing,
Seke in here bed sche lay.
Here fader, her moder come her too,
And gan refrayne here of her woo
To help here yef thei may;
And sche ansuerd withoute wrong,
And seid here payn was so strong
Sche wold sche were loke in clay.

41   The ryche duke, in o mornyng,
And with him many a lording,
As a prince proued in prede,
Thei thoughten hem withoute lesing
Ffor to wend on here huntyng;
Thei bosked hem to ryde.
When all the lordings schuld gon
And went oute of that wordely wone —

39:6 The subject of *kyde* could be either Belesawnt —"She could show it [i.e. her love] to no one"— or *no man*: "no one could/it would be impossible to describe it" [i.e. the extent of her love].

39:7-9 "Whenever she saw him ride or walk past, it seemed to her that her heart broke in two for not being able to speak with the handsome man". Note the impersonal construction *here thought*.

40:12 "She wished she were enclosed in earth", i.e. dead and buried.

41:4 "It came into their mind to go hunting". The plural *thei* is unexpected; the subject must be "the duke and many a gentleman with him" (ll.1-2), despite l.3, where the focus is exclusively on the duke.

In herte ys nought to hide —
Syre Amys, withoute les,
Ffor o maladye that on him wes,
At home he gon to abyde.

42   When all the lordyngs were went
With here houndes and bowe ybent
To hunt on holtys hare,
Syre Amys thoo verament
Belefte at home in present,
To kepe all that there were.
Then the knyght bethoght him thoo
Into a gardeyn for to goo,
Ffor to solace him there;
And under a bought he gan hym hide.
To here the somers song that tyde
Him thought a blysfull fare.

43   Now herkeneth, and ye mow here
How the dukes doghter dere
Seke in here bedd lay.
Here moder come with mornyng chere
With all the ladyes that ther were
Ffor to solace that may.
Sche said: "Doughter, for love myne,
Wyll we wend into the gardyne
This ilke somers day?
There we may here the foules song:
Ffor joye and moche myrth among
Thi care shall all away."

44   Up aroos that berd bryght;
Into the gardeyn scho went ryght,
With maidens hend and free.
That somers day was faire and bryght;

41:9 For *hert*, other MSS read *herd*, "company", "household". As the line stands, it is best understood as a protest of sincerity and truthfulness on the part of the narrator: "In heart [i.e. truly], there is nothing to hide".

42:3 *holtes hare* is an alliterating phrase meaning "ancient woods". Another (less likely) way of reading the line could be that the courtiers go to hunt the hare in the woods.

The sonne schone thorght leme of lyght —
Merye yt was to see!
There herd thei foules grete and smale,
The note of the nyghtyngale
Merye singyng on tree;
Bote here *hert* was so hard ywroght,
On love longyng was all here thoght —
Myth here game *no* glee.

45   Thus, the mayde, in that tyde,
Walked onder that orchard syde
To slake here of here care:
Than sche sawe sire Amys besyde.
Under a bowgh he gan abyde,
To here merthes mare.
Then was that maide blyth;
Here joye cowth no man kyth
Ffor that sche sawe him thare,
And thought sche wold for no man wend
Bote sche wolde to him fonde
To talk him of here care.

46   That maide was so blyth of mode,
No lenger sche ne stent ne stode:
To him sche went, that swete,
And thought for all this world good
To speke with that ferdly food
Ffor no thing wold sche lete.
And astyde as that gentyll knyght
Sey that berd in bour bryght,
He come with here to mete

44:10 *B. here hert w.* - MS *B. here w.*; 44:12 *Myth h. g. no g.* - MS *Myth h. g. ne g.* ; 46:9 *He come* - MS *Come*

44:5 *leme of lyght*: literally, "gleam of light"; i.e. the sun shone with a bright radiance.
44:12 *myth* is here a form of *might*: "No music could please her"
46:9-10 The text as it stands is pleonastic: "He went to meet her and went in her direction". The other MSS readings ("As soon as the noble knight saw the beautiful maiden coming over to meet him, he went towards her"),

And ayens here he gan wende:
With wordes that were free and hende
Well faire he gan here grete.   [17a]

47   Astyde that mery maide anon
      Bede here maydens everychone
      To drawe hem away;
      And whenne thei were hemself alone,
      To sire Amys sche made hire mone,
      And seid withoute delay.
      Sche saide to him "Sire knyght,
      My love ys on the so hard yplyght,
      Eke be nyght and be day,
      But thow wylt my lemman be
      My hert me think wyll breke at three:
      No lenger leve y ne may."

48   "Thou art", sche said, "a gentyll knyght,
      And y a berd in boure bryght,
      And of hight ken ycomen.
      Both be dayes and be nyght,
      My love ys so on the alyght,
      My wytte ys nyghe forloren.
      Plyght me thi trowth thou schalt be trewe,
      And never chaunge for no newe
      That in this world ys born,
      And y schall plyght my trowth also,
      Tell God and deth part us atwoo:
      Y schall not be fornsworn."

49   That hend knyght styll stodde,
      Ffor that he chaunged his mode,
      And seide with wordes free:
      "Madame, for Him that dyde on rode,
      As thou art come of gentyll blode
      And eire of this lond schalt bee,

---

though superior, were not adopted because they would have involved further
emendation.
47 Similar scenes where the heroine actively pursues the hero may be found
in other English romances such as *Horn* or *Beves of Hampdon*; the
passionate heroine is also a regular character in those French romances where
the hero is somewhat lower in rank.

Thenk all on thi moche honour,
How kinges sone ne emperour
Were not to guode for the.
Certeys, then were yt unryght
Thi love to ley uppon a knyght
That hath nother land ne fee."

50 That merye maide of grete renoun
Ansuerd: "Whi had thou not a croun,
Ffor Him that bought the dere?
Wheter art thou preste or chanoun,
Other art thou monk or parson,
That prechest me thus here?
Thou schuld have ben made no knyght
To go among ladyes bryght,
Thou schuld have ben a frere!
He that taught the to preche,
To the devell of hell y him beteche,
My brother thaught he were!"

51 "Ffor, be Him that all this world hath boght,
All this preching helpith the nought,
Stonde thou never so long!
But thou graunte me my thought,
My love schall be well dere ybought
With peynes hard and strong.
My kerchyefs and my clothes echon
Y schall torente hem anon,
And seyn with moche wrong
That thou hast me all todrawe:

49:9 "The son of a king or an emperor": the desirability of the heroine is particularly stressed in the Anglo-Norman romance, where we are told that she was courted by dukes and counts.

49-50 In MS A, the answer of the hero extends over another stanza, stressing the gravity of a breach of vassalic duty (Leach, 601-612):
& yif we schuld that game biginne / & ani wight of al thi kinne / Might it vndergo, / Al our ioie & worldes winne / We schuld lese, & for that sinne / Wretthi God ther-to. / & y dede mi lord this deshonour, / Than were ich an iuel traitour;/ Ywis, it may nought be so./ Leue madame, do bi mi rede / & thenk what wil com of this dede: / Certes, no thing bot wo.

50:2 The croun refers here to clerical tonsure.

51:3 stonde is here a subjunctive: "however long you keep on doing so".

Than schalt thou with londes lawe
Be demyd well hyght to hong."

52   That hend knyght stode stylle
And in herte that lyked ylle.
No word ne saide he thoo;
He thought, but he graunt here wyll,
With here speche sche wold him spyll
Ere than he went here froo.
"And yef y do my lorde that wrong,
With wylde hors and with strong
I schall be drawe alsoo.
Lothe y am that dede to don,
And well lother y am my lyfe forgon."
He was never so woo.

53   Then saide he withoute lesyng,
"Yt ys better to graunt here asking
Then thus my lyfe to spylle",
And seid to that maiden yong:
"Ffor Jhesu love, heven king,
Understond thou my spelle.
As thou art maide guode and trewe,
Thenk hou ofte rape will rewe
And turne to grame with gryll!
Abyde", he said, "this sevenyght;
And as y am trewe knyght,
I schall graunt the thi wyll."

54   Then ansuerd the berd bryght,
And suore be Jhesu full of myght:
"Thou spekest me notte soo!

52:3 Line barred out by scribe (anticipation of l.6).

51:12 "condemned to hang very high". Despite the final *t*, *hight* is an adjective not a verb.
53:4 An elliptical construction: the subject (*he*) is implicit.
53:7-9 MS H has Amys speak to Belissaunt in a more moralising tone: *As thou ert maydyn gent & fre / Thynke how harde thys hap wol be / And turne beter thy wylle.*
54:3,6,9,12 The tail-rhyme scheme is defective in this stanza: lines 3 and 6 do not rhyme with 9 and 12. Moreover *so* (lines 3 and 6) is made to rhyme

Thou schalt me thi trouth plyght,
As thou art a gentell knyght,
Thou schalt hold that so!"
All here wyll he graunted thoo,   [17b]
And plyght here trowthes both twoo,
And kyste that faire may.
Into here chamber sche went agayn;
Off here joye couth y notte sayn
Off that sche made than.

55   Syre Amys, withoute dwellyng,
      To loke upon his lordys yn comyng,
      To the hall he went anon;
      And when thei come fro there huntyng —
      And with hem many a lordyng —
      Into that wordely wone,
      After his doughter he asked swythe,
      And men said sche was glad and blythe,
      Here care was all agoon.
      To mete in halle thei brought that may;
      Glad and blythe sche was that day:
      Thei thanked God everychone.

56   Tho all the lordes, withoute les,
      Henlyche were sette in does
      With ladyes bryght and swete.
      Rychely served thei wes,
      As *princes* that were proued in prees,
      With merthes and *mariness* to mete.
      Thenne that maide that y of tolde,
      Among the barons that were so bold,

56:5 *As princes* - MS *As princers*; 56:6 *With m. and mariness* - MS *With
m. and marners*; 56:11 *hundred* - MS *C*; 57:7 *And be here s.* - MS *And he
here s.*

---

with itself, while line 12 suggests the scribe may have been trying here to
patch up a garbled text — his line 11 is the last of the stanza in the other
MSS.
   56:4-6 *wes* is a Northern form of the preterite plural of "to be": "They were
served richly, like noble princes, with joy and merriness at their meal". The
alliterating expression *proued in prees* may be paraphrased as "splendid in a
crowd".

There sche sate in here sete;
And on sire Amys that gentill knyght
A hundred sythe sche kaste here syght —
Ffor nothing sche wold lette.

57   Uppon sire Amys, that knyght hendye,
Ever more sche kaste here ye:
Ffor nothing wolde sche spare.
Thoo the steward full of felony
Ffaste he gan hem aspye
Tylle he wyste of here fare;
And *be* here syght he saw thoo
Grete love was betwene hem twoo
And therof he was greved sare;
And he thought whithin a lytell while,
With some treson othir with gyle,
To bring hem into care.

58   Thus, ywys, that mery may,
In halle with game and with play,
Ffoure dayes other ffyve,
When that sche sire Amys say,
All here care was away;
Well was here alyve!
Whether that sche sette other stode,
Sche beheld that ferdly foode:
Sche stent for no stryve.
Seth the steward with wordely sake
Brought hem bothe in moche wrake,
That evell mot he tryve!

59   The ryche duke, uppon a day,
On huntyng he went his way,
And with him many a man;
And Belsaunt, that faire may,
To chamber ther sire Amys lay,
Well ryght the way sche nam.
The felle steward in that tyde
Was in a chamber there besyde
And sawe that maide than;

And to here chamber he gan glyde
Ffor to aspye hem that tyde:
Swythe after he ran!

60   And when sche come to that wordely wone,
Syre Amys sche fonde alone,
And grete that swete wyght.
"Sire Amys", sche saide anon,
"This day sevenyght ys agoon
That we oure trewthes plyght.
Therfore y am come to the,
To wytte yef thou be hende and free,
As thou arte a trewe knyght:
Whether thou wylt me forsake
Other thou wylte trewly to take
And holde that thou me hight."

61   "Madame", sire Amys gan to sayn,
"I wolde spouse the full fayn
And holde the to my wyffe:
But yefe thi fader herd sayn
That y hadde his doughter forleyn,
Oute of lond he wold me dryve.
And yefe y were a king in londe
And had more guode into my honde
Than other kinges fyve,
Ffayn y wold wed the than:
But, certes, y am pouer man.
Woo ys me alyve!"

62   Than answerde that maide in mynde:
"Syre, for seynt Thomas love of Ynde,
Whye saist thou ever moo nay?
Were thou never so pouer of kynde,   [18a]

62:12 *E. t. she* - MS *E. t. he*

59:10 Considering the situation, the MS reading (*here*, "their", or "her") is
somewhat surprising; one would have expected *hys* (=MS H).
62:2 According to legend, the Apostle Thomas went to India to preach the
Gospel. The saints by whom the characters swear are significant; Saint
Thomas, the disciple who doubted the reality of Christ's resurrection, is aptly
invoked by Belesawnt to denounce Amys's lack of confidence in her.

51

Bothe be nyght and day."
That hende knyght bethought him than,
And in his armes he here nam
And swete he kiste that may.
And so thei pleide in word and dede
That he wan here maidenhede
Ere than *she* went away.

63   And ever the steward gan abyde
A lytell under the chamber syde
Here councell for to here:
In at a hole that was not to-hide
He saw hem ther in that tyde,
Howe that thei were in fere.
And when he had seyn that syght,
Syre Amys and that berde bryght,
The dukes doughter dere,
Wroth he was and egre of mode;
And awey as he were wode,
Here counseyll to discure.

64   When the duke come in that wone,
The steward ayens him gan gon,
Here counseyll for to wrayen;
And to the duke he saide anon:
"Sire, of thin harme, be seint John,
I wyll the warne full fayn!
In thi court thou hast a thefe
That hath brought my hert in grefe —
Schame yt ys to sayn!

63:11 "And away he went as if he were mad". Our manuscript is isolated in not having a verb precede *awey*; the resulting change in rhythm – whether intentional or not – gives added emphasis to the violence of the steward's reaction. Other examples of increased effectiveness due to metrically defective lines may be found in swift-moving or strongly assertive passages: see for example 69:10 or 81:1.

64:5 The Apostle John, who of all Christ's disciples was the only one to have remained with him at the foot of the Cross, is generally invoked in the poem when characters wish to stress their loyalty; see also 68:4 or 78:4. By contrast, Saint Giles appears when characters are making morally dubious plans; see 78:4. This is not due to the saint as much as to the fact that *Gile* rimes with *guile*, "trickery"; a rhyme also found in the French analogues.

Certes, he ys a traitour strong,
Ffor he with treson and with wrong
Thi doughter hath forlayn."

65   Than wax the duke full of grame:
"Who hath don me that ylk a schame,
Tell me now, y the pray!"
"Syre", he said, "be seynt Jame,
Well y can tell the his name,
And thou wylt hong him this day.
It ys thi boteler sire Amys,
That ever hath ben thi treytour, ywys,
That hath forleyn that may.
I saw myselfe this day, for soth.
I wyll yt preve before hem both,
That thei can yt not forsayn".

66   Then waxe the duke egre of mode,
And ran to the hall as he were wode;
No lenger wolde he abyde,
And with a fauchon scharp and guode
He smote to sire Amys there he stode,
And failed of him besyde.
And into a chamber he sterte him thoo
And schette the dore betwene hem twoo,
Ffor drede his hed to hyde;
And he smote after with a dent,
That thorought the dore the fachon went,
So egre he was that tyde.

67   And all that ever aboute him stode
Besought him to slake of his mode,
Both knyght and swayn.
He swor by Him that dyed on rode:
"Y wold not for this worldys guode

65:4 The steward is swearing by Saint James the Greater, whose shrine at
Compostella was one of the most famous centres of pilgrimage of the Middle
Ages.
65:6 The *and* can here be understood either as "and" or "if".
66:6 "And missed him narrowly". The pronouns in this stanza are
somewhat confusing; however, the context makes it clear that *he* refers to the
duke in ll.1-6 and 10-12, and to Amys in ll.7-9.

Bote that tretour were yslayn!
I have don him moche honour,
And, certes, he ys a foule treitour!
My doughter he hath forlayn:
I wolde not for all this worldys won
But y myght that treitour slon
With my hondes twayn!"

68   Than said sire Amys anon:
"Sire, lete thi wrath overgon,
Ffor Goddys love, y pray the!
Yef thou myght wyt, be seint John,
That y have suche a dede ydon,
Dampne me to honge on tree.
But who that hath with wrong
Ilyen on us that lesing strong,
What baron that he be,
I schall preve yt in bataile
He lyeth on us withoute faile:
I schall make us quite and free."

69   "Ye", saide the duke, "Wylt thou soo?
Darest thou batell with him doo,
Yow quite and clere to make?"
"Ye, certes sire", he seid thoo,
"Here my glove redy therto!
He lyeth on us with wrake."
The steward, fast to him he ran,
And seid: "Treitour, thou fals man!
Ateynt thou schalt be take!
I saw yt myselfe this day,
Where togeder that ye lay —
Non of you may yt forsake!"

70   Thus the steward ever gan say,
And ever sire Amys saide nay:
No wonder thowgh here were wo!
Than he lette fette that may;

68:4 "If you can know for sure": for *wyt*, the other MSS read *preve*,
"prove", a technical term more in keeping with the situation.
   70:4 *he* is here the duke.

The steward, withoute delay,
Avowed the dede also.
That mayd wepte and here honds wrong,   [18b]
And ever swore the moder among:
"Certes, yt ys notte soo!"
Then said the lordings without faile:
"It schall be preved in bataill
And *sen* betwene hem twoo."

71   Thus betwene hem thei toke the fyght
        And sette that day a fortenyght,
        That many man schuld yt sene.
        The steward was so moche of myght,
        In all the court was ther no wyght
        Syre Amys borowe to bene;
        Bote for the steward was so strong,
        Borowes anon he fond among,
        Twenty all bedene.
        Than seide thei all with ryght reson,
        Sire Amys schulde be yn preson,
        That he schulde not faile.

72   Than ansuerd that berde bryght,
        And swore, "Be Jhesu full of myght,
        That were moche wrong!
        Take my body for that knyght
        Tell the day be come of fyght,
        And doth me in preson strong.
        Yef that knyght flee away
        And dare not hold up his day
        Batell of him to fonde,

70:6 *Avowed* - MS *aswonde*; 70:12 *And sen* - MS *And seth* ; 71:10-11
Inversion marks in margin

70:7 *honds* must be read *hondes*; metre demands an unstressed syllable
between *honds* and *wrong*.
71:12 "So that he should not fail [his word]". The line makes sense, but
faile does not fit into the rhyme scheme, and appears to be a misreading of
flene, "flee" (= MSS A,S,H).
72:9 "To engage in battle with him" In view of the rhyme scheme of the
stanza, MS *fonde* is probably an error for *fonge*, the reading of the other
MSS.

Batell of him to fonde,
Dampneth me with londes lawe
Ffor his love bien todrawe,
And hight on galows to hong."

73 Than spake here moder wordes bolde
And seide gladly that sche wold
Be his borow right alsoo
That he, as a guode knyght, schuld
That day of batell upholde
To fight with his foo.
Thus this ladyes faire and bryght
Bede for that gentyll knyght
To leyn here bodyes twoo.
Than seide the lordyngs echon:
"Other borows kepe we non".
Thei graunted yt schuld be so.

74 When thei had, as y you say,
Ffound borows for that may
And graunted all that *ther* were,
Sire Amys morned nyght *and* day.
All his joye was went away,
Ycome was all his care;
Ffor the steward was so strong,
And had the ryght and he the wrong,
That he on him bare.
Off his lyfe he nought rought,
But on that maide moche he thought:
Myght no man morn mare,

74:3 *all that ther were* - MS *a.t. the were*; 74:4 *nyght and day* - MS *nyght day*

72:9 "To engage in battle with him" In view of the rhyme scheme of the stanza, MS *fonde* is probably an error for *fonge*, the reading of the other MSS.

74:2 "When they had [...] found sureties for that maiden": this is technically incorrect, since the securities are for Amys, not Belesawnt. Other MSS, instead of *for that may*, read *withouten delay* (A), *for/til that day* (S,H). MS *may* could therefore be an error; the original text probably read *delay*, since *day* reappears as rhyme-word in l.4.

56

75 Ffor he thought he moste nede,
  Ere than to the batell he yede,
  Swere an oth beforn,
  As wissely God schuld him spede
  As he were gyltles of that dede
  That on him was boren;
  Than thought he withoute wrong
  He had lever be drawe and hong
  Than to be forsworn.
  Ofte he besought Jhesu thoo
  He schuld schild hem both twoo,
  That day thei were not forloren.

76 And as sire Amys went to play,
  He mette that lady and that may
  In that orchard syde.
  "Sire Amys", the lady gan say,
  "Whye mornyst thou nyght and day?
  Tell me the soth this tyde."
  "Drede the nought", sche saide than,
  "To fyght ayen thi foman:
  Wheter thou go other ryde,
  So rychely y wyll the schrede
  That thou dare him never drede,
  Batell of him to abyde."

77 Than ansuerd that knyght,
  "Madame, for Jhesu love full of myght,
  Be not wroth for this dede:
  I have the wrong and he the ryght.
  Therfore y am aferde to fyght,
  As God me mote spede,
  Ffor y mote swore withoute faile,
  As God me spede in my batayle,

75:1-6 These lines explain the statement made on line 74:12, and provide the terms of the oath the hero has to swear, in reported speech — "For he reflected that he was compelled, before going to battle, to swear an oath: [That] God would protect him, as certainly as he was innocent of the deed he was charged with".

75:12 *were* is here a subjunctive: "so that they be not lost on that day". The loss that is referred to is not only physical death, but also damnation (See 77:11).

That yt ys falshede.
And yef y swore, y am forsworn:
Lyffe and soule y am forloren.
Certes, y can no rede."

78   Than seid that lady in that while:
"Sire Amys, can thou no gyle
To bring that traitour adoun?"
"Yes, dame", he seid, "be seint Gyle!
Here woneth hens three hundred myle
My brother sire Amylyon,
And yefe y durst to him gon,
Y wold swore be seint John,
So trewe ys that baron,
His own life to lay to mede,   [19a]
He wold her help me in this nede
To fyght with that felon."

79   "Sire Amys", that lady gan say,
"Aryse tomorn when yt ys day,
And wend in thi jurne.
I schall be thi warant, yef y may,
And that thou art to thi contray
Thi fader and moder to see;
And when thou comest to him ryght,
Pray him, as he ys a gentyll knyght
And hold hende and free,
That he the batell underfong
Ayen the steward, that wyth wrong
Wolde overcome us all three."

80   Amorn, sire Amys dyght him yare
And toke his leve for to fare,
And went in his jurnay.
Ffor nothing he wold spare:
He preked the stede that him bare,

78:5 *three hundred* - MS *iii* C

78:4,8 The emblematic quality of the saints invoked by Amys is especially
obvious here; see note 64:5.

79:5 "[I shall be your warrant] that you have gone to your country": the
past participle is implicit.

Both be nyght and day.
So long he preked withoute abode,
That the hors that he on rode,
In a faire contray
Was overcome and fill doun dede.
Tho couth the hend knyght no rede;
His song was "Welawey!"

81   Seth yt befill soo,
Nethes he moste afote go:
Karfull was that knyght!
He toke up his lappes loo,
And in his way he ran forth tho,
To holde that he byhight.
All that day as he nam,
Into a wylde forest he cam,
Betwene day and nyght.
Grete sleppe ran him uppon;
To wynne all the worldys won,
No further he ne myght.

82   That hende knyght, that was so free,
Laide him faire under a tree,
And fill aslepe that tyde.
All that nyght, stylle lay he,
Tyll amorowe: ne myght he se
The day be every syde.
Then his brother, sire Amylyon,
Was a lord of grete renoun
In all that contre wyde,
And woned fro thens that he lay
But halfe a jorne of a day,
Other to goo other ryde.

83   And as sire Amylyon, that gentyll knyght,
In his bedde lay anyght,
A dreme he mette anon.
Him thought he saw sire Amys with syght,
His brother that was trowth plyght,

81:4 *his lappes loo*: literally, "his low hems". Amys is tucking up his long
riding clothes, which would have hampered his progression on foot.

Lapped among his fon,
With beres that were egre of mode,
[And wolves that were wyld and wode:
Beset he was to slon,
And he alon among hem stode]
As a man that coude no gode.
Well wo was him bygoon!

84   And when sire Amylion gan to awake,
Grete mornyng he gan make,
And tolde his wyffe full yare
How he sawe bestys bloo and blake
Aboute his brother with moche wrake
To sle him with sorow and care;
"Ffor certes", he seid, "with som wrong,
My brother ys in perell strong;
Of blysse he ys all bare."
And then he seide: "Ywys,
I schall never have blysse
Tell y wytte how that he fare!"

85   Astyde, he sterte up in that tyde:
No lenger wold he abyde,
But dyght him redy anone.
His folk aryse up in eche syde
And busked hem redy to ryde,
With here lorde to gon.
Than bade he all that there was
Schuld be stylle and hold her pees,
And abyde at home echone;
And swore, be Him that schope mankynde,
With him schuld no man wende
But himselfe alone.

86   Rechely he gan him schrede
And lept uppon a well guode stede;
No lenger wold he abyde.

83:8-10 Supplied from S - om. MS; 84:1: *Amis* corrected by scribe into *Amylion*

All his folk he gan forbede
None were so hardy of dede
To folow him that tyde.
All nyght he rode tell yt were day,
Tell he come there sire Amys lay,
Into the forest wyde.
Then sawe he a wery man forgon,   [19b]
Leying under a tre; anon
To him he gan ryde.

87   When he come to him full ryght:
     "Aryse felawe, yt ys lyght,
     And tyme for to goo!"
     Sire Amys brayde up with his syght,
     And sone he knewe that gentyll knyght;
     And he dede him also.
     The gentyll knyght, sire Amylion,
     Off his stede lyght him adoun,
     And kyste togeder both two.
     "Brother", he said, "what dost thou here,
     And lokest thus with sory chere?
     Who hath wroght the this woo?"

88   "Brother", seid syre Amys thoo,
     "Me was never so woo
     Sygh that y was boren.
     Fforsoth, the tyme thou wenst me froo,
     With joye and myrth also,
     I served my lord byforen;
     Now the fell steward, with envy,
     With gyle and with trechery,
     Hath do me this sorow on;
     And but thou help me at this nede,

86:4-5 "To all his retinue, he forbade that any of them be so daring as to
follow him". The syntax is potentially confusing here due to the absence of a
relative pronoun. The subjunctive in l.5 is required by the verb of command.

86:11 For *anon*, the other MSS read *alon*. For our MS reading to make
sense, we must postulate that *anon* qualifies the verb of the following line
("Immediately, he rode towards him").

87:6 "And he recognised him too". The verb *know* of the preceding line is
implicit.

61

Certes, brother, y can no rede.
My lyffe y have forloren."

89   "Brother", seid sire Amylion,
"Whi hath the steward, that felon,
Don the thus moche schame?"
"Certes", he seid, "with treson
He wolde bryng me adoun,
And hath do me moche grame!"
And he told him the cas
How he and the maide was
Togeder both insame;
And how the steward hem bewrayn,
And how the duke wold him han slayn,
With wrath and with grame.

90   And he told him plyght
How he had take that fyght,
Batell of him to fonge;
And how in court was no wyght
Save the two ladyes bryght
Durst be his borow among,
And how he most swore, withoute faile:
"As God me spede in my bataile!
Yt were a lesyng strong,
And a forswore man schall never *spede*.
Certes, brother, y can no rede;
Alas may be my songe!"

90:10 *spede* - MS *spde*; 91:8 *bay* deleted in MS before *batayle*

89:6 For *grame*, the other MSS read *blame*, which avoids the repetition of
the same word at the rhyme

90:8 This line may be understood in two different ways. It could be an
exclamation —"May God assist me in my battle! That would be a great
lie"— in which case one may note the irony of Amys's formulation of his
dilemma; the "great lie" precludes any hope that God assist him in combat.
Alternatively, the line may be read as the continuation of 1.7, echoing the
terms of the oath Amys has to make: [He told him how he had to swear] "As
truly as God will assist me in battle". The corresponding passage in A
(Leach, 1090-1100) is less problematic: *& hou he most, with-outen faile, /
Swere, ar he went to bataile.*

62

91   And when sire Amys had ytolde
        How the felle steward wolde
        Bring him adoun with mode,
        Syre Amylion spake wordes bold
        And swore, "Be Hym that Judas solde
        And dyde uppon the rode,
        Of his hope he schall faile!
        And for the, y wyll take the batayle,
        Thoght the treytour be wode;
        And yef y may mete him aryght
        With my brond that ys so bryght,
        I schall se his harte blode!"

92   "Thou schallt have, brother, all my wede,
        And in thi robe y wyll me screde,
        Ryght as thi selfe yt were;
        And y schall swere, so God me spede,
        That y am gyltles of that dede
        That men on the bare."
        Thus the hend knyghtes twoo
        All here wede chongyd thoo,
        That thei were well yare.
        Then said sire Amylion: "Be seint Gile,
        Thus y schall the schrew begyle
        That wold my brother forfare!"

93   "But thou schalt wend home full ryght
        To my lady faire and bryght,
        And do as y schall seyn;
        And as thou art a gentyll knyght,
        Lye with here abed anyght
        Tyll y come agayn;
        And sey thou hast sent thi stede, ywys,
        To thi brother, sire Amys,
        Ffor he wyll be therof fayn.
        Thei schull wene that y yt be,
        Ffor no man schall know the,
        So lyke be we twayn."

---

93 The instructions of Amylion are here very different from those given in
the *chanson de geste*, where he absolutely forbids any sexual contact with his
wife Lubias. Amys's chastity is therefore all the more commendable.

94   Syre Amylion, that gentyll knyght,
Went in his jurney;
And sire Amys went home full ryght
To this lady fayre and bryght,
Withoute more delay;
And seid he had sent his stede
To his brother worthi in wede,
Be a knight of that contray.
Then wend thei all, up and doun,   [20a]
That hyt were here lord sire Amylion,
So lyke were thei twoo.

95   Then sire Amys, full yare,
Tolde hem all of his fare.
Well thei wend thoo,
Lytell and moche, lesse and mare;
And all that ever in courte were
Wend yt had ben soo.
And when ycome was the nyght,
Sire Amys and the lady bryght,
To bedde gon thei goo.
And when thei were in bedde layd,
Sire Amys his swerde oute braide,
And leid yt betwene hem twoo.

96   The lady loked on him thoo,
Wordely, with here yen twoo,
And wend here lord were wode.
"Sire", sche said, "whi farest thou so?
Thus were ye never wont to doo!
Who hath turned thi mode?"

94:12 Rhyme demands that *twoo* be read *tway*.

95:3 This line has no expressed object, possibly by error; we have to go to
1.6 to complete the construction. The meaning, however, is clear: everyone
believes what Amys says.

96:2 As is often the case in our MS, the *d* of *wordely* corresponds to our *th*.
The word, as it stands here, is best translated as "worthily" or "in a dignified
way", and could suggest concern on the lady's part. This reading, however,
may be due to metathesis; the other MSS read *wrothlich*, "angrily", a
reaction more in keeping with the character such as we find it in the French
romance.

64

Than he seid: "Sekerlie,
Y have on me suche maladye
That all chaunged ys my blode;
Ffor all my bonys be so sare,
I wolde not nye thi body bare
Ffor all this wor*ldes* guode."

97   Thus, ywys, that gentyll knyght
Dwelled in that court plyght,
As lorde and prince in prede.
But he foryate never anyght:
Betwene him and that lady bryght,
His sworde he laide besyde.
The lady thought in here reson
That here lord sire Amylion
Had ben seke that tyde;
Therfore sche hild here styll thoo
And thurst speke a word nemo,
But thought his wyll to abyde.

98   Nowe herkeneth, hende! Y will you say
Howe sire Amylion went his way.
Ffor nothing wolde he spare:
He preked both nyght and day,
As a knyght stoute and gay.
To courte he come full yare,
That selve day, withoute faile,
That was sette of that batayle.
Syre Amys was notte thare;
Then were the ladyes take in honde
Here jugement to underfong,
With sorow and syking sare.

99   The steward hoved on his stede,
With spere and scheld, batell to lede.
Grete boste he gan to blawe,
And to the duke well sone he yede,
And seid: "Syre, so God me spede,
Herkenyth to my sawe!

96:12 *wordles* - MS *worldes*

The tratour ys oute of londe ywent:
Yefe he were here in present,
He schuld be hong and drawe.
Therefore, y aske jugement,
That his borows ben brent
After londis lawe."

100   The ryche duke, with wrath and wrake,
      Comaunded the ladyes to take,
      And bryng hem forth besyde.
      A strong fere he hete make:
      A tonne thei brought for there sake,
      To brenne them that tyde.
      Then thei loked in to the feld;
      Thei sawe a knyght with spere and scheld
      Come prekyng with prede.
      Then seid thei: "Forsoth, ywys,
      Yonder cometh ryding sire Amys!",
      And bede them to abyde.

101   Sire Amylion stent at no ston,
      But preked among hem everychon,
      And to the duke he gan wende.
      "My lorde duke", he saide anon,
      "Lete thou this ladyes goon —
      Thei ben both guode and hende —
      Ffor y am come hider today
      Ffor to help hem, yefe y may,
      To brenge hem oute of bende.
      Ffor certes, yt were moche unryght
      To make roste of ladyes bryght;
      Iwys, ye are unkynde!"

102   Then were the ladyes blythe;
      Here joye couth no man kythe,
      There care was all away.
      And as ye may leste and lyth,
      Into ther chamber thei went swyth,

101:12 "Indeed, you are cruel". *unkynde* is much stronger that the modern "unkind"; it bears connotations of perverse cruelty, and literally means "unnatural".

66

Withoute eny delay;
And richely thei gan him schrede
With helme and plate and worthi wede.   [20b]
His tyre, yt was full gay;
And when he was on his stede,
That God allmyghti schuld him spede
Many man bade that day.

103   And as *he* rode oute of the toun,
A voys then come fro heven adoun,
That no man herde bote he,
And saide: "Knyght, syre Amylion,
God that suffred passion
Sent the worde be me:
Yefe thou this batell underfong
Thou schall have aventure strong
Withine this yeres three.
Ere than the iii yere ben agon,
A ffouler man was never non,
Certes, than thou schalt be."

104   "But, for thou art hend and free,
Jhesu the sent worde by me
To warn the anon.
A more wrecche than thou schall be,
In care, in sorowe and poverte,
Was never man worse begon.
In all thi londe faire and hende,
Thei that are thi best frende
Schull be thi moste fon;
And thi wyffe and all here ken
Schull schonye the stede that thou art inne,
And forsake the everychone."

103:1 *And as he r.* - MS *And as r.*

103-104 In the French analogues, the warning comes later and is connected with the betrothal rather than the battle. On the implications of this, see Introduction, pp.5-7.

104:10 "Your wife and all her kin": for *here*, the other MSS read *thy*, "your", which emphasizes the extent of Amylion's future loneliness, but is incorrect, since Oweys is explicitly said to be related to the hero.

105   The hend knyght stode styll aston,
        And herde these wordes everychone,
        That were so hard and grylle.
        He wyst not what was best to don,
        To flee or to batell gon;
        In herte he lyked ylle.
        He thought: "Yf y beknow my name,
        Then schall my brother go to fame —
        With spyte thei wyll him spyll."
        "Certes", he saide, "for drede of kare,
        To save my trowth wyll y not spare:
        Lette God do his wyll!"

106   Then thei wend all, ywys,
        That yt had ben sire Amys,
        That batell schulde there abyde.
        He and the fals steward, ywys,
        Were brought before the justys
        To swere for that dede.
        The steward swore the people among,
        As wys as he saide no wrong,
        God schuld helpe him at his nede.
        Sire Amylion swore that ilk day,
        As he never had that may,
        Oure Lady schuld him spede.

107   And when thei had sworn, as y told,
        To beker the barons were full bold,
        And busked hem to ryde.
        All that ther was, yong and olde,
        Besought God that Judas solde
        Schuld save the knyght that tyde.
        On stedes that were styffe and strong
        Thei ride togeder with schaftes long.

107:8 *Thei r.* - MS *To r.*

106:8-12 The terms of the oaths sworn by the two characters are given in
reported speech. In both cases we have the same syntactical structure: "As
truly as he said no wrong/ had never possessed that maiden, God/Our Lady
would help him". The somewhat crude reading of l.11 (*had*) is replaced in the
other MSS by a more euphemistic *kist* ("kissed", MS A) or *nyghed*
("approached", MS S).

Thei *scheverede* be every syde;
Then thei drewe swerdes guode
And hewe togeder as thei were wode:
No lenger wold thei abyde.

108   The knyghtes that were egre of syght,
With fachons felle thei gon fyght,
And ferd as thei were wode.
So hard thei laid on helmes bryght
Sterne dentes of moche myght,
The fere before outestode;
So long thei hew on bak and syde,
Thorght dent of grymely wondes wyde,
All thei spraid on blode.
Ffro morow to none, withoute lettyng,
Thei stent never of fyghtyng,
So egre thei were of mode.

109   Sire Amylion, as fere on flynte,
To the steward with wrath he went,
And smote a dent wyth mayn.
Of him he failed of his dent;
The stede unto the erth went
And smote oute all the brayn.
The stede fyll dede doun to ground:
Wo was the steward in that stound,
Ffor fere he schuld be slayn!
Sire Amylion lyght of his stede,
And to the steward well faire he yede,
And halp him up agayn.

110   "Aryse", he saide, "steward, anone!
Nedys thou moste afote gon,
Ffor thou hast lore thi stede:
It were grete schame, be seint John,
Ye a lying man to slon,
That ys falle in nede!"

107:9 *Thei scheverede* - MS *Thei schonerede*

107:9 "They broke to pieces on each (i.e. both) sides": *thei* refers to the long shafts mentioned in the preceding line; the *thei* of l.10 refers once again to the combatants.

Sire Amylion was free to-fonde   [21a]
And toke him up be the honde,
And seid, "So God me spede,
Nowe thou schall afote goo,
And fyght y wyll afote allsoo;
And els yt were falshede."

111   So togeder thei fyght than,
        The steward and the dowty man,
        With brondes bryght and bare.
        So hard thei hew togeder than
        That here armour all of blode ran:
        Ffor nothing wolde thei spare.
        The steward smote him that stonde
        In the scholder a grymely wounde
        That greved him full sore;
        Thorow that wound, as ye may here,
        He was know with rewly chere,
        After when he fyll in care.

112   Sire Amylion for wrath wex wode
        That all his armour ran of blode,
        That was so white as swan;
        And with a fachon sharp and guode,
        He smote the steward ther he stode,
        As a dowty man.
        Into the breste the sworde gan wade,
        Then by the schulder blade,
        And to his herte yt ran.
        Thoo the steward fill doun dede,
        And sire Amylion smote of his hede,
        And God he thanked than.

113   And all the lordyngs that ther were,
        Lytell and moche, lesse and mare,
        Thanked God that tyde.
        He dyght him and made him yare;
        The hed uppon his spere he bare —

111:10-12 "It is through that wound, as you may hear, that he was
recognised with sadness after he had fallen into misfortune". This anticipates
stanza 171, where it is Amylion's wound, not his cup, that allows Amys to
recognise him.

70

No lenger wold he abyde.
Thei lad him into the toun
With a fayre processioun,
And went by every syde;
And after *lad* him into the towre,
Wyth moche joye and moche honour,
As lorde and prince in prede.

114 When he was in the paleys gon,
All that was in that wordely wone
Wend sire Amys yt were.
"Sire Amys", said the duke anon,
"Here, afore my barons everychone,
I graunte the here full yare
Belesawnt that faire may,
Ffor thou hast bought here love today
With grymely woundes sare.
Therfore, y graunt the now here
All my lond and my doughter dere,
To hold for evermore."

115 Then ansuerd that gentyll knyght,
And thanked him with all his myght,
Ffor glad was he, and fayn;
And in the court was no wyght
That wyste whate his name hight,
Save the ladyes twayn.
Leches thei had sone yfounde;
Thei gon taste the knyghtes wound,
And heled him faire agayn.
Then were the ladyes fayn and blythe,
And thanked God a hundred sythe
That here steward was slayn.

113:10 *And after lad* - MS *And after had*; 114:7 MS *Ffor B.*; 115:11
hundred - MS *C*

115:6 This detail (that the ladies knew the true identity of their champion)
is proper to the English romance. The French analogues further stress the
resemblance of the two heroes, whom even the passionate Belissant cannot
distinguish from one another.

116   And after, sire Amylion dyght him yare,
       And toke his leve for to fare
       To wende in his contray,
       To telle his frendes that there were,
       Lytell, moche, lesse and mare,
       How he spedde that day.
       The duke yaf him leve that tyde,
       And bad knyghtes with him ryde;
       And he answerd and sayd, nay,
       With him schuld no man gon
       But he himselfe alon;
       And went forth in his way.

117   In his way he went alone;
       Ne myght no man with him gon,
       Nether knyght ne swayn;
       Ffor that dowty knyght of blode and bone,
       He never stent at no stone
       Tyll he come home ayayn.
       Sire Amys, than, as y you say,
       Wayted his comyng every day
       In that forest playn.
       When thei come togeder insame,
       He told him with joye and game
       How he had the steward slayn,

118   And how he schuld for that dede   [21b]
       Spouse that mery maide to mede,
       That was so comely born.
       And sire Amylion lyght of his stede,
       And there thei chonged ayen here wede,
       As thei dide beforn;
       And bade him go to court ayen,
       And taught him whate he schuld sayn
       When he come ther thei weren.
       Then was sire Amys glad and blythe,

117:11 *He told* - MS *To tell* ; 118:11 *hundred* - MS *C*

118:9 "When he came where they were". It is not clear who *thei* refers to. It could refer to the people at court; or possibly, it could be a reference to the heroes' shared experience at that same court in the past. S has a simpler *When he theder com wore.*

And thanked God a hundred sythe
The tyme that he was boren.

119 When thei asonder schuld wende,
Sire Amylion, that knight so hende,
Home he went that tyde
To his lady riche of kende;
And he was honourd of his frende
As lorde and prince in prede.
And when yt was come to nyght,
Sire Amylion and the lady bryght
In bed lay him besyde;
And in his armes he gan here kysse,
And made here moche joye and blysse —
No lenger he wold abyde!

120 And the lady asked him thoo
Whi he had faren soo
All that fourtenyght,
And whi he laid his sword betwene hem two,
That sche ne durst, for wele ne woo,
Nyght his body aryght.
Sire Amylion bethought him than —
His brother was a trew man,

118-119 MS A has here another stanza, where Amys vows to requite his friend's help at any cost (Leach, 1441-52):
& *when thai schuld wende ato | Sir Amis oft thonked him tho | His cost & his gode dede. | "Brother", he seyd, "yif it bitide so | That the bitide care other wo, | And of min help hast nede, | Sauelich com other sende thi sond, | & y schal neuer lenger withstond, | Al so God me spede; | Be it in periil neuer so strong, | Y schal the help in right & wrong, | Mi liif to lese to mede".*

119:4 Instead of the positive *riche of kende*, "of powerful kin", A reads *that was unkende*, which anticipates the role of Amylion's wife later in the narrative.

119:9 Amylion and his wife "lay in bed beside each other": *him* is a variant form of the plural *hem*.

120:6 The lady did not dare to "approach his body properly/ at all": this line refers to the absence of any sort of physical contact between the lady and Amys, but the connotations here are more especially sexual. This is in keeping with the characterization of women (in all versions of the story) as lascivious.

And had so don, aplyght ! —
And seid, "Madame, y wyll the sayn,
And the sothe tell the full fayn:
But wray me to no wyght."

121 Alstyde the lady to him say gan,
Ffor His love that this world wan,
To tell here whi yt were;
And anon, the dowty man
All the sothe tell here he gan:
And to court how he dede fare,
And how he slew the steward strong
That wold with treson and wrong
His brother have brouth in care;
And how Amys, that gentyll knyght,
Lay with here abedde anyght
While that he was thare.

122 Than woxe that lady wroth, aplyght,
And ofte mysseid here lorde that nyght,
With spise betwene hem two;
And seid: "With wrong and with unryght
Thou slew there a dowty knyght:
It was well evell ydo!"
Then said he: "By heven kyng,
I dede yt for none other thing
But to save my brother fro woo;
And I hope, yefe y had nede,
His own lyfe to lye to mede
He wolde for me alsoo."

123 Herkeneth! Now y wyll you sayn
How sire Amys was glad and fayn,
To court when he schulde wende;
And when he come to court agayn,
With erle, baron, knyght and swayn,
Well honourd was that hende.
The ryche duke toke him by the honde

120:9 This line may be understood in two ways: "[His brother was a loyal man] and he had acted loyally indeed", or "[His brother was a loyal man] if he had so acted, indeed". The implications are quite different. For *And*, the other MSS read a less ambiguous *That*.

74

And seysed him in all his londe,
To hold withoute ende;
And afterward, uppon a day,
He spoused Belsaunt, that may
That was so trew and kynde.

124　So, withinne yeres twoo,
A well faire grace fyll hem thoo,
As God allmyghty yt wolde:
The duke, here fader, dyed hem froo,
And here moder dyed allso,
And were graved in cloddes colde.
Then was sire Amys, hende and free,
Duke and lorde of grete postee
Over all that lond yhold;
And two childerin begate on his wyve.
Ffayrer were none alyve,
In geste as yt ys tolde

125　Then was sire Amys of grete renoun,
And lord over towre and town,
And duke of grete poste;
And his brother syre Amylion,
With sorow and kare dryven adoun,
That ere was hende and free.
As the angell had him ytolde,　　　　　　　　　　　　[22a]
A fouler lazar was none yholde
In this world then he.
To rede in geste, yt ys grete rewthe,
Whate sorow he had for his trewthe
Withinne the yeres three!

126　Ere than the iii yere were go to ende,
He wiste never whider to wende,
So wo was him begon.
In all the lond faire and hende,
Tho that were his best frende
Become his moste fon;

125:5 "[Amylion] with sorrow and care was driven down": the verb is
implicit.
126:4-5 "Those who were his closest friends became his worse enemies".
MS A reads here *For al that were his best frende / & nameliche al his riche*

And his wiffe, as y you say,
Wrouth him worst every day
Than thei dyde everichon.
And when him was befall that cas,
A frendeles man than he was.
A lyves man wysched he were non!

127 So wikked and schrewed was his wiffe,
Sche brake his herte withoute knyffe,
With wordes hard and kene;
And seid to him: "Wrecched kaytyf,
With wrong the steward lost his lyfe,
That ys nowe well ysene!",
And swore: "Be seint Denys of Fraunce,
Therefor thou hast this myschaunce,
Thaugh who the bemene."
Many a tyme his hondes he wrong,
As a man that thought his lyfe to long,
That ys in trey and tene.

128 Alas for that gentyll knyght
That whilom was so faire and wyght
And than brouth so woo!
Oute of his own chamber, anyght,
Ffro his lady faire and bryght,
[He was yhote to goo;
And out of his halle a day

126:9 *everichon* - MS *everchon* ; 128:6-8 Supplied from S - om. MS

---

kinde, which reintroduces the notion of the failure of blood-ties and family solidarity.

127:7 According to legend, the martyred Saint Denis picked up his severed head and walked off with it; the oath of Amylion's wife thus betrays her desire to see her husband dead, but also prefigures the miracle which will enable the cleansed leper to return home.

127:9 "Despite whoever may lament you". MS A has a much stronger *Dathet who the bimene*, "Cursed be whoever pities you". The attitude of Amylion's wife towards her husband's illness appears to have been common; see BRODY, esp. pp.60-106.

128:6-8 The scribe of our MS has omitted these lines, possibly because of the similarity in meaning of ll.6 and 9, which allows the stanza to make sense despite the lacuna.

Ffro the hyghe bord, y yow say,]
He was chased alsoo.
To eten at the monthes ende
Wolde no man sytte him be hende:
Carfull was he thoo!

129   When the halfe yere was ygo
That he had eten in hall thoo,
With guode mete and drynke,
The lady woxe wrath and woo
That he leved so long soo,
And seid, withoute lesyng:
"Yef in my lond spring that worde
Y fede a lazar at my borde
That ys so foule a thing,
It ys grete spite to a ladys kende.
He schall no more sytte me hende,
Be Jhesu heven kyng!"

130   And on a day sche gan him call
And seid: "Yt is so befall,
Ffor soth y tell yt the,
It ys grete spite to us all
That thou hast ben so long in hall.
My kynne ys wroth with me."
The knyght wept, and seid here tyll:
"Dame, do me there ys thi wyll,

128:10 "By the end of the month no one was willing to sit next to him to eat": we have here the suggestion of a gradual process from the moment Amylion's affliction becomes obvious to all. The other MSS stress the hero's debasement, with *at the dormand ende* (MS S) and *at the tables ende* (MS A) instead of *at the monthes ende*. The high table, so called because it was frequently on a dais, was reserved for the nobler diners; at the other tables the seating was determined by rank, the places of honour being at the top end, and the "worse" seats being at the opposite extremity. Amylion is thus treated like the most menial member of the household.

129-131 Even though the audience is clearly meant to sympathize with Amylion and condemn the lady, one may note that this procedure was the usual one for people afflicted with leprosy. If anything, Amylion's wife has been unduly lax in allowing a leper to remain so long in her court. Leprosy was equivalent to social death, and lepers theoretically had no right to own property; this explains Amys's reaction (*It were ayens the lawe!*, 165:3) when he hears that a leper has a cup as precious as his own.

That no man me ne se.
Of no more gode y the pray,
But o meles mete every day,
Ffor seint charyte."

131   The lady, for here lordes sake,
        Astyte dede men tymber take:
        Ffor nothing wold sche wonde.
        A pryve logge sche did make,
        Halfe a myle fro the gate,
        Oute of the way to stonde;
        And when the chamber was wrouth,
        Of all his gode he asked nought
        But his golde cuppe in honde;
        And when he was therin alone,
        To Jhesu Cryste he made his mone,
        And thanked Him of his sonde.

132   And when he was in that logge dyght,
        In all the court was no wyght
        That wold him serve there,
        Save a gentyll child, yplyght;
        Child Oueys his name hight:
        Ffor him he wept well sare.
        The childe was trew and of his kende,
        His suster sone; he was hende.
        To him he seid full yare
        That he never wold wonde
        To serve his lorde, a fote and honde,
        While he alyve were.

132:9 *his suster sune*: this extremely close kinship of Oweys and Amylion is a characteristic of the English versions. The Anglo-Norman poem merely states that the child is *Fiz de un counte, son parent* (l.825), "the son of a count, a relative of his".

132:11 *a fote and honde*: i.e. completely, in all possible ways. The hands and feet may here refer either to Amylion's (which Oweys will wait upon), or to Oweys' own (he will serve his lord with both hand and foot).

133   The childe that was so faire and bold,
          [Of twelf wynter he was old,
          Certes, hende and good;
          And trew he was, as y yow told.]
          Ffro his lorde, never he wold,
          So kende he was of blode;
          And in his chamber anyght he lay,   [22b]
          And to court he went every day,
          To feche here lyves fode;
          Ffor myght him never glad no song,
          But ever for his lord among
          He wepte with drery mode.

134   Tho he went every day
          Ffor to feche here leveray:
          Ne stent he for no stryfe.
          All that ther was gan him pray
          To come fro the lazur away —
          Then he schulde the better thryfe.
          The child ansuerd with myld mode
          And swore by Him that dyde on rode
          And suffred woundes fyve:
          "Ffor all this worldys guode to take,
          My lord schall y never forsake
          While that y am alyve!"

135   Withinne that the xii monthes were gon,
          He went to the wordely wone

133:2-4 Supplied from S - om. MS

133:2-4 MS A gives the boy both a name and a nickname, as in the Anglo-Norman romance (Leach, 1634-7): *Owaines was his name ytold / Wel fair he was of blode / When he was of tvelue yere old / Amoraunt than was he cald.* Compare with the Anglo-Norman romance, 880-882: *Le noun vous dirray de l'enfant: La gent l'appelent Amorant, Mes Uwein fuit son dreit noun,* "I shall tell you the name of the child: he was called Amorant, but his real name was Uwein".
133:5 "To go from his lord he would never consent".
133:10 *glad* is here a verb: "No song could cheer him up". Our MS is isolated in reading *Ffor*; MS S reads *Ne*. In MS A, Amorant is contrasted with those surrounding him (Leach, 1642-4): *When ich man made gle & song / Euer for his lord among / He made dreri mode.*

79

To feche here leveray.
The lady woxe wroth anon,
And bade here men everychone
To take the childe away;
Sche swore be Him that Judas sold,
Though here lorde for honger and cold
Dyde ther that he lay,
And swore, be Jhesu heven king,
Have he schuld mete, ne drynk, ne nothing,
Ffor here after that day.

136   And child Oueys went home agayn
And wepte and wrong his hondys twayn,
With sorow and syking sare.
Anon, the gode man gan him frayn,
And bad he schulde him sayn
And tell him whye yt were.
"O, Sire", he said, "be seint John,
No wonder thaugh me be wo begon —
My hert wyll breke for care!
Thi wife hath sworn with here mode
That sche wyll never do the gode.
Alas, how schuld we fare?"

137   "O Lord", said that gentyll knyght,
"While that y was man of myght
To dele mete and cloth;
And now y am so wreched a wyght,
All that se me nowe with syght,
My lyfe wexith them loth.
Therfor let be, sone, thi weping;
This ys nowe a evell tything,
That may y sey for soth.
Therfore, certenly, y can no rede,

135:7-12 A difficult construction. The point made by the lady is interrupted by the repetition of her oath (*Sche swore ... and swore*), with the result that the sentence appears to be disjointed. This may be intentional: it emphasizes the blasphemous quality of the lady's oath, while the syntactical incoherence suggests her agitation and anger.

137:2 "At one time I was a powerful man". *while that* must be understood as a compound conjunction synonymous with *whilom*.

But go to town and bey oure brede.
Iwisse, therto yt goth."

138   And erly amorn, when yt was lyght,
Child Oueys and that gentyl knyght
Dyght hem redy anone:
In here wey went forthryght
To bey here mete, as thei had tyght,
Ffor brede had thei none.
So long thei went, up and doun,
Into a guode cheping town
Ffyve myle oute of that wone;
At every hond thei gon prove
To begge here mete for Godys love,
Ffor evell couth thei theron.

139   Then woxe the knyghtes fete so sare
That he myght no further fare,
Ffor all this worldys guode;
To the townes ende the child him bare,
And a logge he dobbed him thare
As folk to cheping yode;
And he come to cheping every day,

138:10 "On every side they tried ...". Instead of *hond*, MS S reads *hous*, thus depicting Amylion's haphazard begging as a systematic door-to-door strategy.

138:12 This line is best translated as: "It was because of their ill fortune that they brought themselves to do it" (literally, "knew how to do it"). The other MSS read *Ful iuel* (A) and *Iuel* (S), which Leach (p.127) understands as "Very wretchedly they had knowledge therein".

138-139 MS A has an additional stanza at this point, describing their success at begging and their relative comfort and happiness (Leach, 1705-1717):

So in that time, ich vnderstond / Gret plente was in that lond, / Bothe of mete & drink; / That folk was ful fre to fond / & brought hem anough to hond / Of al kines thing; / For the gode man was so messaner tho / & for the child was so fair al-so / Hem loued old & ying, / & brought hem anough of al gode; / Than was the child blithe of mode / & lete be his wepeing.

This follows neither the Anglo-Norman romance nor the *chanson de geste* and is in contradiction with the beginning of stanza 140, which stresses their *care and poverte*.

139:7-9 Lines 7 and 8 are inverted as compared to the other MSS (cf. MS S: *As the folk of that contray / Com to chepeing eueri day / Thai gat hem*

As the folk of that contrey,
To gete hem lyves fode;
And ofte the child to town gan go
And gate hem mete, and drink also,
When hem moste nede stode.

140   Thus in jeste rede wee,
Thei dwelled there yeres three,
The child and he also;
And leved in care and poverte
By the folk of that contre,
As thei come to and fro.
So, within the fourth yere,
Corn began to wex dere:
Honger began to goo.
Ther was nother olde ne yong
That wolde gefe him mete, ne nothing.
Well carefull were thei thoo!

141   Childe Oueys to town gan gon;
Mete ne drinke gate he non,
Ne at man ne wyve;
And when thei were togyder alone,   [23a]
Ffull rewly thei made here mone,
That wo was hem on lyve.
Then, his wiffe, as y you say,
Woned there in that contray
Thense but myles ffyve,
And leved in joye nyght and day
Whiles that he in care lay;
Well evell mote sche thryve!

142   And on day, as thei were alone,
That hend knyght gan make his mone
To the childe in that tyde;
And, "Sone", he seid, "thou most gone
To my lady, now anone,
That woneth here beside.
Bede her, for Him that dide on rode,

---

liues fode). As a result, instead of describing Amylion's sedentary begging,
these lines refer to the activity of Oweys in securing food for both of them.

Send me so moche of my guode
As an asse uppon to ryde,
And oute of londe y wyll fare
To begge my mete with sorow and sare:
No lenger y will abyde."

143   Anon the child to court went,
Tofore his lady faire and gente,
And seid to here anone:
"Madame", he seid, "verrament,
As a massanger my lord me sent,
Ffor himselfe may not gon
And you besouche with milde mode
To send him so moche of his guode,
On asse to ryde uppon;
And oute of londe we schull wende,
Schull we never come the hende,
Though honger schuld us slon."

144   The lady saide sche wold fayn
Sende him guode asses twayn
With that he schuld gon,
"So that ye never come agayn".
"Nay, certeys", the childe gan sayn,
"Thou seist us never here more."
The lady lowe and wexe blythe,
And comaunded asses swythe,
And seid to him thoo:
"Now ye schull of londe flene:
God yeve you neve: to come ayen,
And graunte that yt be soo!"

145   This child his asse gan bestryde;
No lenger he wolde ther abyde,
But went him home agayn,

143:5-7 "My lord sent me as a messenger, for he himself cannot come to humbly beseech you...".

144:8 "And ordered strong asses [be brought]". Other MSS only mention one ass here (cf MS A, & comaund him an asse as swithe), despite the lady's statement that she will give two. In the Anglo-Norman romance also, only one ass is mentioned; but no promise is made by the lady to give more than what was requested of her.

And told his lord in that tyde
How his lady proud in pryde
Schamefully gan sayn.
On the asse he dyght that knyght so hende
And oute of town thei gon wende.
Then were thei glad and fayn;
In that contre, up and doun,
Beggyd here mete fro town to town
Both in wynd and rayn.

146   In that contre, with Goddys wyll,
Honger ther waxe harde and gryll,
And asse with asse thei gon go.
Almost for faint thei gon spill:
Thei had no brede halfe here fill.
Carfull were thei tho!
Then said the knyght upon a day:
"Us behoved selle oure asses away.
We have guode no mo
But my ryche cuppe of golde
That schall never be solde,
Thaught honger schuld me slo."

147   Child Oueys and sire Amylion,
With sorow and rewly ron,
Erly in on mornyng
Thei come to a cheping town.
There, the knyght lyght adoun
Withoute more dwellyng;
The child in the town gan go,
And toke with him the asses two,
And sold hem for v shilyng;
And while the honger was so strong,
Therwith thei bought her mete among,
When thei myght gete nothing.

145:11 The subject (*thei*) is implicit.

146:3 Instead of the mention of the asses, the other MSS read here *As wide as*, thus stressing the extent of the famine.

146:8 Despite the final *-ed* of *behoved*, the verb is in the present tense: "We have to sell our asses away".

148   When the asses were solde
Ffor v schilyng, as y you tolde,
Thei dwelled there dayes three.
Then was child Oueys stoute and bolde;
Off xv wynter he was olde,
Certes, hende and fre.
Ffor his lord he had grete care;
At his regge he dyght him yare,
And bare him oute of that cite.
Halfe a yere and sumdele mare,   [23b]
Aboute his mete he him bare:
Yblessed mote he be!

149   Thus the child, as y you say,
Served his lord every day,
And at his regge he him bare;
And ofte his song was "Welaway",
So wyked and schrewd was that contray.
His lemes were full sare.
Then was all here catell spent,
Save xii pens, verrament.
Therewyth he went well yare,
And bought him a guode croudwayne;
Therin he gan his lord layn —
He myght bere him namare.

150   Then crouded the child sire Amylion
In all the contre, up and doun,
As ye may understonde,
Tel he come to a cheping town
There sire Amys, that bolde baron,
Was duke and lorde in londe.

148:6 For *certes*, MS A reads a more conventional *curteis*.

148:8 He [Oweys] willingly put him [Amylion] on his [Oweys'] back.

148-149 MS A has an additional stanza at this point describing the hardships endured by Owein/Amoraunt (Leach, 1837-48):

Thus Amoraunt, with-outen wrong / Bar his lord about so long / As y you tel may. / That winter com so hard & strong / Oft, "Allas!" it was his song / So depe was that cuntray; / The way was so depe & slider / Oft times bothe to-gider / Thai fel doun in the clay. / Ful trewe he was & kinde of blod / & served his lord with mild mode, / Wald he nought wende oway.

This has no parallel in the French versions.

Then saide the knyght in that tyde:
"The dukes court ys here beside;
Will we theder fonde,
Ffor he ys a man of mylde mode.
We schull gete there some guode,
Thorow grace of Goddys sonde."

151 "But leve sone", he saide than,
"Ffor His love that love wanne,
As thou art hende and free,
Loke thou wray me to no man,
Whider y will, ne when y came,
Nether whate my name be."
The child ansuerd and seid, "Nay".
To court he crouded him in that way,
As ye may lythe at me,
And forth be all the poure men,
He crod hem ryght into the fen:
Grete dole yt was to se.

152 That tyde befyll upon a day,
With tonge as y you tell may:
It was myd-wynter tyde.
The ryche duke, with game and play,
Ffro chirche he came in that way,
And as lorde and prince in prede;
And when he come to the castell gate,
Pouer men that were there ate,
Thei drew him besyde.
With knyghtes and serjauntes fale,
Ibrought he was into the sale,
With joye and blysse to byde.

153 In kinges court, yt was the lawe
Trompettes schulde to mete blawe;
And to benche thei yeden bold.
When thei were sette on rawe,
Served thei were, as ys the lawe,

151:2 "For the love of He who won love"; this is an unusual way of
referring to Christ, and is probably a misreading for the more conventional
"For the love of He who redeemed this world" (*that this world wan*; cf
121:2).

As men meryest on molde.
The ryche duke, withoute les,
As prince that was proud in pres,
Served he was with golde:
And he that brought him to that state,
He stode besteked withoute the gate,
Well sore hongred and colde.

154   And oute of the gate ther come a knyght,
And a serjaunt wise and wyght,
To pley hem both in fere.
And thorow the grace of God Almyght,
On sire Amylion he caste hes syght,
How loth he was of chere.
Also, he beheld his servaunt,
How he was gentyll and avenaunt,
In jeste as ye may here.
Then seid thei both, be seint John,
In all the courte wes ther non
Off fairehed halfe his piere.

155   The guode man to him gan go,
And hendely asked him tho,
As ye may understonde,
What contre that he come fro,
And whi that he stode there so,
And whome he served in lond.
"Sire", he saide, "So God me save,
I am here my lordes knave,
That lyeth in Goddes bonde.
And as thou arte jentyll man of blode,
Bere oure arend of summe gode,
Ffor the grace of Goddys sonde!"

156   The guode man asked him anon
Yefe he wolde fro the lazar gon,
And trewly to him take;
And he schuld serve, be seint John,
The ryche duke of that wone.

154:3 "To amuse themselves". The *guode man* of stanzas 155, 156 and 157
is the knight.

A man he wolde him make.   [24a]
The childe ansuerd with myld mode,
And swore by Him that dyde on rode:
While he myght walke and wake,
His lord that he over stode,
To wynne all this worldys guode,
He wold him never forsake.

157   Then wend the guode man that he dide rage,
       Or he had ben full savage,
       Or his wytte had ben forloren;
       Or he thought that he with the foule visage
       Had ben a man of grete parage,
       Other of hight kenne yborn.
       Therfore he wolde no more sayn,
       But went into the halle agayn,
       The ryche duke beform,
       And seid, "Lord, lestne to me!
       The best bourde, so mote y the,
       Thou herdest sen thou were born!"

158   The duke comaunded him anon
       To tell before hem everychone
       Withoute more dwellyng.
       "Sire", he saide, "be seint John,
       Oute of the gate y was gon,
       Ryght now in my playng.
       Pouer men then fond y thare,
       Lytell, moche, lasse and mare,
       Both olde and yong;
       And a lazur ther y fond —
       Herd y never, in no lond,
       Speke of so foule thing!"

158:2 *everychone* - MS *evychone*

156:10 "His lord, over whom he was standing ...": a touch of realism, since Amylion is indeed sitting at Oweys' feet in his wheelbarrow. MS A reads here *his hende lord that bi him stode* (Leach, 1943).

157:2 MS A reads for *full savage, fole-sage*, which Leach (p.128) understands as meaning "jester", "court fool".

157:10-11 "Lord, listen to me, to the best joke you ever heard ...".

159   "The lazur lyeth in a wayn,
And ys so pouer of myght and mayn,
Afote ne may he nat gon;
And over him stant a naked swayn.
A gentyler child, for soth to sayn,
In this world ys non.
He ys the fairest ycome
That ever had Crystendome,
Other lyfe layde uppon:
And the moste fole he ys
That y herde speke, ywys,
Within this worldle won!"

160   The duke ansuerd him ayen
"What foly, *he seyd,* gan *he* sayn?
Is he mad of mode?"
"Sire", he said, "y gan him frayne
To leve the lazar in the wayne
That he over stode:
I bede him both gold and fee
In thi service for to be,
And have of worldly guode.
And he ansuerd and seid, na,
He wold never his lord fra.
Therfore y hold him wode!"

161   Then seid the duke: "Wherever he be born,
Paraunter the guode man here beforn
Hath holp him at his nede,
Other he is of his kend boren,
Other he hath othis to him sworn
His lyfe with him to lede.
Wheter he be of his blode,
The child ys both trew and guode,
As God me mote spede!
And for he is trew and kynde,
Yef y speke with him er he wende,
I schall aquite his mede."

160:2 MS *With foly cause gan sayn*

161:7 "Whether or not he is of his blood...".

162   The riche duke that y of told
        Cleped to him a squier bold,
        And hendly gan him sayn
        He schuld take his cuppe of gold
        As full of wyne as he myght hold
        In his hondes twayn,
        And bere yt to the castell gate.
        "A lasur thou schall fynd therate,
        Layng in a wayn.
        Bede him, for the love of seint Martyn,
        He and his page drynke that wyne,
        And brynge the coppe agayn."

163   Anone the squier the cuppe hente,
        And to the castell gate he wente,
        And full of wyne yt bare.
        To the lasur he said verrament:
        "This wyne my lorde the sent;
        Drynke yt yefe thou dare."
        The lasur drew forth his cuppe of gold —
        Both were yoten in on molde,
        As that selfe yt were.
        Than helte he the wyn so ryche;
        Then were thei both lyche,
        Nether lasse ne mare.

164   The squier behelde the cuppes two,
        Ffyrst his, and his lordes also,
        Whyle he stode him before;
        But he ne couth never mo   [24b]
        Chese the better of the two,
        So lyke bothe thei waren.

162:10 Saint Martin of Tours is best known in popular piety for having divided his cloak to share it with a beggar, but his legend also mentions that he embraced and cured a leper. It is therefore fitting that he should be invoked in connection with an act of charity to the leper Amylion.

163:6 "Drink it if you need", rather than "if you dare"; this is not a challenge on the part of the squire. See Glossary, **dare.**

163:11-12 "Then they were both the same, neither being smaller or bigger than the other": the pouring of the wine from one cup to the other has shown that beyond the fact that they are identical to look at, they also hold the same amount of liquid.

Into the hall he gan ayen;
"Certeys, lorde", he gan seyn,
"Moche guode thou hast forloren,
And so thou hast this dede nowe,
Ffor he is rycher man than thowe,
Be the tyme that God was boren!"

165   "Schall he never, be nyght ne day!
It were ayens the lawe!"
"Yes, certes", he gan sey,
"He ys a treytour, be my fay;
He were worthi to be drawe.
I toke him the cuppe with wyne:
He drew oute another, as fyne
As yt were thyn awe.
In all the world ther is non
So wyse a man, be seint John,
Asonder schuld them knawe!"

166   "Certes", said sire Amys tho,
"In this world were cuppis nomo
So lyke in all thing,
Save myn and my brothers also,
That was set betwene us two
In tokne of oure partyng.
Yef yt be so, with sume treson,
My hende brother, sire Amylion,
He is gyled withoute lesyng,
And he have stole his cuppe away.
I schall him sle this ilk a day,
Be Jhesu heven king!"

165:1 *The duke a.* - MS *The a.*

164:9-10 "You have lost much property, and you have just now wasted this good deed".

165:2 "It would be against the law": lepers lost the right to private property. This legalistic reflex is not found in the Anglo-Norman romance.

166:9-10 Depending on how the reader punctuates these lines, *and* may mean either "and" ("He [Amylion] has been deceived, without lying, and he [the beggar] has stolen his [Amylion's] cup") or "if" ("He [Amylion] has been tricked. If he [the beggar] has stolen his cup [I shall kill him] ").

167 Ffro the borde he sterte than,
   And hent his sword as a wode man,
   And brayd yt out with wrake;
   And to the castell gate he ran.
   In all the court was no man
   That myght him overtake;
   To the lasur he sterte in the wayn,
   And hent him in his hondes twayn,
   And slang him in the lake,
   And trad on him as he were wode,
   That all that ever be him stode
   Grete sorow thei gon to make.

168 Then was the duke egre of mode;
   Ther was no man aboute him stode
   That durst on him ley his honde.
   He sperned him with his fote,
   And leid on him as he were wode
   With his gremely bronde;
   Be the fete he him drowe,
   And trad on him in the slowe.
   Ffor no man wold he wonde,
   And seid, "Traytour, thou schall be slawe,
   But thou the soth wyll me knawe
   Where thou the cuppe fonde!"

169 Child Oueys stode the people among,
   And sawe his lorde, with moche wrong
   How rewly he was dyght.
   And he was bothe stefe and strong:

167-168 The parallel between the behaviour of the duke in the first part of the poem and that of Amys here is striking. MS A has an additional stanza at this point, where Amys questions the beggar (Leach, 2077-88):

"Traitour!" seyd the douke so bold, / "Where haddestow this coupe of gold / & hou com thou ther to? / For bi him at Judas sold / Amiloun, mi brother, it hadde in wold / When that he went me fro!" / "Ya, certes, sir", he gan to say, / "It was his in his cuntray, / & now it is fallen so; / Bot certes, now that icham here, / The coupe is mine, y bought it dere, / With right y com ther to".

In the Anglo-Norman romance, the exchange between Amys and Amylion only takes place after Amis has tired himself out hitting the beggar; and Amylion's response to his friend's questions is a request for a swift death.

The duke in his armes he fong,
And held him streight upryght.
"O Sire", he said, "thou art unkynde,
And of thi workes thou art unhende!
Thou sleyst a gentyll knyght:
Sore may he rewe that stounde
That ever he toke for the that wounde,
To save thi lyfe in fyght!"

170   "And ys thi brother, sire Amylion,
That whilom was a noble baron,
Bothe to ryde and go,
And now with sorowe ys dreve adoun.
Nowe God, that suffred passion,
Breng him oute of his wo:
For the of blysse he ys bare,
And thou yeldyst him all with care,
And brekest his bones atwo,
That he halp the at thi nede.
Well evell aquitest thou his mede:
Alas, whi farest thou so?"

171   When sire Amys herd him thus sayn,
To the knyght he sterte agayn
Withoute more delay,
And hent him in his armes twayn.
Ffor sorow he wepte with his yen,
And seid, "Welaway!"
He loked on his schulder bare,
And saw a grymely wounde sare,
As child Ouys gan say.
Ffor sorow he fill swonyng to grounde,
And seid, "Alas, that ilk stounde
That ever y bode this day!"

172   "Alas!", he said, "My joye ys loren!
Unkender blode was never boren;
I ne wote whate y schall do!

170:10 The main verb is the *yeldyst* of l.8: "You are repaying him [the fact] that he helped you ... with sorrow and by breaking his bones".

172:2 "There was never born more unnatural blood", i.e. a being more cruel than himself.

I ne wote whate y schall do!
He that saved my lyfe beforen,
I have yeld yt him soren,   [25a]
And wrought him nowe well wo!"
"Brother", he said, "par charyte,
This gylt foryefe thou me,
That y have smete the so!"
And he foryafe yt him als swythe,
And kyste togeder a hundred sythe,
Wepyng both two.

173   Then was sire Amys full fayn;
      Ffor joye he wept with his yen.
      His brother he hent than,
      And lapped him in his armes twayn,
      Tell he come to the halle ayan;
      Moste him help no man.
      The lady in the hall stode,
      And wende here lorde were wode,
      And ayens him sche ran.
      "Sire", sche saide, "whate ys thi thought?
      What hast thou in the hall brought,
      Ffor Him *that* this *worlde* gan?"

174   "O Dame", he seid, "be seint John,
      No wonder thaught me wo begon,
      Yefe thou wilte understonde!
      A better knyght in the world ys non
      Than almoste y have slon
      And shamely dryve to schonde!
      It is my brother, sire Amylion,
      With sorow and care dryve adoun,
      That ere was fre to fonden!"
      The lady fyll aswoun to grounde,
      And wept and seid, "Alas that stounde!",
      Sore wryngyng here honden.

175   As foule a lasur as he was,
      The lady kiste him in that plas:

172:11 *hundred* - MS *C*; 173:12 *F. H. that this worlde gan* - MS *F. H. this
worldle g.*

94

Ffor nothing wold sche spare,
And many tyme said, "Alas,
That ever him fyll that ylke cas,
To leve in sorow and care!"
Into a chamber thei dide him lede,
And dyde of all his pouer wede,
And baded his body all bare.
And soth him in the *bedde* brought,
With clothes ryche and well wrought;
Ffull blythe of him thei were.

176   Thus in jeste, as y you say,
       xii monthes in here chamber he lay;
       Trew he was and kende.
       Whate he asked, nyght other day,
       Thei wolde him brenge withoute nay:
       It was never behynde.
       Of every mete and every drynke
       That thei had, withoute lesynge,
       Thei had on him guode mynde;
       And er the xii month were agoo,
       A faire grace befill him thoo,
       In jeste as so we fynde.

177   So yt befill uppon a nyght,
       As sire Amys, that gentyll knyght,
       In his bedde layn,
       He thought, before his bed ryght
       That ther come an angell bryght
       And to him gan sayn:
       Yefe he wold ryse a Crystes morn,
       At whiche tyme as God was born,
       And sle his childerin twayn,
       And smere his brother with the blode,
       Thorow grace of God that ys so guode,
       His care schuld awayn.

175:10 *in the bedde b. - MS in the bathe b.*

175:8 "And took off all his poor clothes".

178   Sire Amylion thought, that nyght also,
        That an aungell come him to,
        And warned him full yare
        Yefe his brother wold his childerin slo,
        The *herte* blode that come hem fro
        Schuld bryng him oute of care.
        Amorn, sire Amys, that was so hende,
        To his brother he gan wende,
        And asked him of his fare.
        And he answerd with wordes styll,
        "I abyde Goddes wyll:
        Thus may do no man mare."

179   As thei sate togider thare,
        And spake of auntres, as thei ware,
        The hende and that fre,
        Sire Amylion said him full yare:
        "Brother, y wyll not spare
        To tell the my pryvyte.
        Tonyght, as y lay in my swevene,
        An angell come to me fro hevene;
        Ffor soth, y tell the,
        With the blode of thi childerin two
        I my skape oute of my wo,
        All hayle and hole to be."

180   Then thought sire Amys, withoute lesing,
        To sle his childerin that were so yong,
        It were a dedely synne;
        Then thought he, be heven king,   [25b]
        His broder oute of care to bryng,
        Therfore wolde he not blynne.

178:5 *The herte b. - MS And with the b.*

177-178 MS A has at this point an additional stanza which triplicates
Amys's vision, a feature found neither in the Anglo-Norman romance nor in
the *chanson de geste* (Leach, 2209-2220):
Thus him thought al tho thre night / An angel out of heuen bright / Warned
him euer more / Yif he wald do as he him hight / His brother schuld ben as
fair a knight / As euer he was biforn / Ful blithe was sir Amis tho / Ac for
his childer him was ful wo / For fairer ner non born / Wel loth him was his
childer to slo / & wele lother his brother forgo / That is so kinde ycorn.

96

This fill on Crystes own nyght,
Whiche tyme as Jhesu full of myght
Was born to save mankynde.
To chirche went all that ther wes;
Thei dyght hem, withoute les,
With joye and worldely wen.

181   So when thei ware all yare,
Syre Amys bade all that thar ware,
To chirche that thei schuld wende,
Lytell, moche, lesse and mare,
That no man lefte in chamber thare,
As thei wolde ben his frende.
He seide he wold himselfe, aplyght,
Kepe his brother, that gentyll knyght.
Ther was no man durste say nay,
But at home belefte that hende,
That was both trew and kende,
And to chirche thei wente here way.

182   The duke full faste gan aspye
The kayes of the norcery,
When thei schuld won,
And prevely he caste his ye,
And saw hem well wytterly
Wher thei were layd anon
When thei were in that tyde
Go to chirche ther besyde.
At home belefte he alone,
And with a candell that was lyght,
To the kayes he yede ryght,
And toke hem away echone.

183   Alone himselfe, withoute mo,
To *the* chamber he gan go
Ther his childerin were,
And he beheld hem both two,

183:2 *To the c.* - MS *To his c.*

181:9-12 Our scribe has inverted lines 9 and 11, and lines 10 and 12 (cp.
MSS A and S). This disrupts the rhyme-scheme of the stanza, but also has as
consequence the shifting of the praise of line 11 from Amylion to Amys.

How faire thei leyn togeder tho,
And pleyde both in fere.
Then said he, "Be seint John,
It ys grete routh you to slon,
That God hath bought so dere!"
His knyfe he had drawen that tyde;
Ffor sorow he stode hem besyde,
And wepte with reuly chere.

184   When he had wept there he stode,
Anon he turned ayen his mode,
Withoute more delay:
"My brother that was trew and guode,
Ffor *me* he sched his own blode
To save my lyfe on day;
Whi schuld y than my childerin spare
To bryng my brother oute of care?"
"Certes", he said, "nay;
My brother to help at this nede
Jhesu yeve me well to spede,
And Mary that best may!"

185   No lenger he ne stent ne stode:
He drew his knyfe with drery mode.
His childerin he hent tho,
And for he wolde not spille here blode,
Over a basyn faire and guode,
Tho throtes he karfe atwo.
And when he had slon both twayn,
In bed he laid hem agayn —
No wonder thow him were wo! —
And held hem faire ayen.

184:5 *Ffor me he s.* - MS *Ffor he s.*

183:8 For *routh*, MS S reads *synne*, which lends a different dimension to
Amys's sacrifice. The scandalous nature of Amys's gesture in S is further
emphasized by the fact that the revelation of the angel is called a *hap*
(176:11), as opposed to our text's *grace*.
    185:10 "And fairly beheld them again". One may also read *helde* as a variant
for *hilde*, in which case lines 10 and 11 belong to the same sentence: "And he
covered them again in a fair manner, as if no one had been there".

As no man had ther yben,
Oute of the chamber he gan go.

186   When he was oute of the chamber gon
He schut the dore, as styll as ston,
As faste as yt was beforen.
The kayes he layd sone anon,
That thei schuld wene everychone
That thei were forloren.
To his brother he went than,
And seid to the carfull man,
"Suche tyme as God was boren,
I have the brought my childerin blode.
I hope yt schall do the guode,
As the aungell seid beforen."

187   "Brother", sire Amylion gan say,
"Hast thou slayne thi childerin tway?
Alas, whi dost thou so?"
He wepte and said "Welaway,
I had lever tyll domysday
Have leved in sorow and wo!"
"Brother", said sire Amys, "be stylle.
God may, when yt ys his wylle,
Send me childerin mo.
Ffor me of blysse thou art bare:
Iwys, my lyffe y wyll not spare
To bring the now ther fro."

188   He toke the blode that was so bryght   [26a]
And anoynted therwith that gentyll knyght,
That ere was hende in halle;
And when he had don, in plyght,
Into a bedde he was dyght,
With clothes ryche and falle.
"Brother", he said, "ly nowe styll,
And fall aslepe thorowght Goddys wyll,
As the aungell seid in tale.
Then y hope, withoute lesyng,
Jhesu, that ys heven king,
Shall bote the of thi bale."

189   Sire Amys lefte him alone,
          And into his chapell he gan gone,
          In jeste as ye may here;
          And for he had his childerin slone,
          To Jhesu Cryste he made his mone,
          And besougth Him, with rewly chere,
          Schuld schild him fro schame that day,
          And Mary His moder, that best may,
          That was lyefe and dere.
          Jhesu Cryste, in that stede,
          Well He herde the knyghtes bede,
          And graunted him his prayere.

190   Amorn, astyde as yt was day,
          His wyffe come homeward in that way
          With knyghtes and ladyes ffyve,
          And sought the kayes ther thei lay.
          Thei fonde not hem: thei were away.
          Wo was hem alyve!
          Then bade he all that there wes,
          Thei schulde be styll and hold here pes,
          And stente hem of here stryve;
          And seid he had the kayes nome.
          In his chamber schuld no man come,
          Bote himselfe and his wyve.

191   Alone he toke his lady than
          And seid to here, "Leve lemman,
          Be blyth and glad of mode:
          Ffor be Him that this worlde wayn,
          Both my childerin y have slayn,
          That were so faire and guode.
          Tonyght, as y lay in my swevene,
          An aungell tolde me, of hevene,
          Thorow oure childerin blode
          My brother schulde be brought oute of wo.

191:8 *An a.* - MS *And a.*

189:11-12 S has here an additional line: *Though the beseching of His mother dere.* The miracle is thus attributed to the Virgin.

Therfor y slow hem both two,
To help that ferly fode."

192 Then was the lady ferly wo,
And so here lorde was also,
And conforted him well yare.
"Syre", sche said to him tho,
"God may send us childerin mo;
Ffor hem have thou no care.
And yefe yt were at my hert rote
Ffor to bryng thi brother bote,
My lyffe wold y not spare.
Ther schall no man oure childerin sen,
For tomorn thei schull beryed ben
As thei faire dede were."

193 Thus that lady faire and bryght
Conforted here lorde with here myght,
As ye may understonde;
Sen thei went both ryght
To sire Amylion, that gentyll knyght,
That ever was fre to-fonde.
When sire Amylion awaked tho,
All his foulehed away was go,
Thorow grace of Goddes sonde:
Then was he as faire a man
As ever he was er than,
Sen he was born in londe.

194 Then were thei all blythe;
Here joye couth no man kythe —
Thei thanked God that day!
As ye mowe at me leste and lythe,
Into the chamber thei went swythe,
Ther as the childerin lay.
Withoute wem, withoute wounde,
All hole the childerin ther thei founde,

192:1-2 "Then was the lady extremely sorrowful, and she saw that her lord
was as well". *so* is here a form of the verb "see" (cp. MS A *seiye*).

192:4,6 Instead of *sire*, MS A reads *O lef liif*, "My dear life", thus
suggesting a less formal and more affectionate relationship between the
couple.

And lay togeder in play.
Ffor joye thei *wept* ther thei stode,
And thanked God with mylde mode:
Here care was al away!

195   When sire Amylion was hole and fere,
        And was wox of strong puere
        Both to go and ryde,
        Childe Oueys was a stoute squire;
        Blythe and glad he was of chere
        To serve his lorde besyde.
        Then saide the knyght uppon a day,
        He wolde wende to his contray
        To speke with his wiffe that tyde;
        And for sche halp him at his nede
        He wolde aquite here mede.
        No lenger he wold abyde.

196   Sire Amys sent full hastelye
        After many a knyght hardy
        That dowty were of dede,
        Well five hundred kene and thre,
        And other barons bold him be,
        On palfray and on stede.   [26b]
        He pryked both nyght and day
        Tyll he come to his contray
        There he was lord in dede.
        Then had a knyght of that contre
        Spoused that lady bryght of ble,
        In jeste as we rede.

197   Bote thus, in jeste as y you say,
        Thei come home that ylk a day

194:10 *thei wept* - MS *thei went*; 196:4 *five hundred* - MS *v C*

195:10-11 "And because she had helped him when he was in need, he would repay her her reward". This is of course grim sarcasm.

196:4 "A good five hundred and three bold men"; or, in view of the instability in our manuscript of *th*, *d* and *t*, *thre* could be a form of the adjective "true" (cf. MS S: *try*).

196:5 *him be*: "in addition to them", i.e. to the five hundred knights; or "accompanying him". MS S reads "by and by" (Leach, 2441).

That here bredale was holde.
To the gate thei preked withoute delay;
And ther gan wax a sory play
Among the barons bolde!
A messanger to halle was nome
And seide here lorde was home come,
As man meryest on molde.
Then woxe the lady blak and wan;
There was many a sory man,
Both yonge and olde!

198 Sire Amys and sire Amylion,
And with hem many a stoute gerison,
With knyghtes and squiers fale,
With helm on hede and habergon,
With brondes both bryght and broun,
Thei went into that sale;
And all that thei ther *raughte*,
Grete strokes there thei *caughte*,
Both grete and smale.
Glad and blythe were thei
Who that myght skape away,
And fle fro that bredale!

199 When thei had with wrake
Drove oute both broun and blake
Oute of that wordely won,
A strong logge he dide make,
Sire Amylion, for his lady sake,
Bothe of lyme and stone.
Therin was the lady led;
With brede and water sche was fed,
Tell here lyve dayes were done.
Thus the lady was brouth to deth
As a wreche full of quethe,

198:7 *raught* - MS *laste*; 198:8 *caught* - MS *causte*

198:7-8 "And all those that they could reach, they received great blows".
199:11 "Like a wretch full of evil". In MS S, we have here an intrusion of
the narrator: *Who therof rought, he was a queede* (Leach, 2483). This
conventional curse echoes that of the lady when she discovers Amylion's
illness.

As ye have herde echone.

200   Then sire Amylion sent his sonde
After erle, baron, fre and bonde,
Both faire and hende.
When thei were come, he seised in honde
Childe Oueys in all his londe,
That was both trew and kende;
And when he had don this, ywysse,
With his brother sire Amys,
Ayen he gan home wende.
In moche joye, withoute stryfe,
Togeder lad thei here lyfe,
Tell God wolde after hem sende.

201   Anone, this hende barons twey,
Thei lete make a guode abbey,
And well yt afefed tho,
In Lombarde that contraye,
To sing for hem tyll domysday,
And for her eldres also.
Both on o day thei bothe dyde,
And in on grave thei were leyde,
The hende knyghtes both two;
And for ther trewth and here guodehede,
The blysse of heven thei had to mede,
That lasteth ever moo.

Amen, for charyte!

Explicit vita de Amys et Amylion

201:9 *The hende k.* - MS *That hende k.*

200:4-5 "When they were come, he put Oweys in possession of all his land".

Appendix 1.

Rodulfus Tortarius, "Ad Bernardum".

Summary of lines 123-320, OGLE and SCHULLIAN pp.260-7.

The two heroes are born in Gaul, Amelius in Auvergne, at Clermont, and Amicus in Gascony, at Blaye. The youths, both of outstanding beauty and prowess, go into service at Poitiers, at the court of the King Gaiferus; there they vow indissoluble friendship to each other. Not even death will subsequently separate them, since they are both buried at Mortaria near Vercelli. The youths enjoy great favour at court when Beliardis, the daughter of the king, falls passionately in love with Amelius. Their illicit affair arouses the envy of one of the courtiers, Ardradus, who denounces them to Queen Berta. The infuriated queen demands Amelius's execution; but the king, who is upset by this calumny of his daughter and does not want to condemn a man without judgement, allows Amelius to defend himself in judicial combat. Amelius then decides to consult Amicus, who was absent at the time, on what to do; and the two friends decide to take advantage of their great physical resemblance to exchange places. Amicus will fight with Ardradus, while Amelius stays with Amicus's recently married wife, who is not aware of the substitution. However, Amelius avoids all fleshly contact with his friend's wife by placing a sword between them at night, much to her disappointment. At court, Amicus can rightfully deny the charge made by Ardradus that "the man here present dishonoured Beliardis"; he eventually emerges victorious from the judicial combat, thanks to the sword of Roland, given to Gaiferus by Charlemagne, and handed over by Beliardis to her swordless champion at a critical moment of the battle. Ardradus is killed, and Beliardis is given to Amelius/Amicus. The young couple go to visit Amicus/Amelius, the heroes exchange their clothing once again, and both couples live happily for many years. But then, Amicus becomes a leper. His wife cruelly banishes him from the town in a cart drawn by one mule, and with only one servant; Amicus thus becomes a beggar. But at Clermont, he is recognised by Amelius who welcomes him despite his affliction, and gives him personal care. Amelius asks doctors about possible cures for his friend's illness, and is told that the only remedy is children's blood. He then sends away Beliardis, kills his own children, and cures Amicus with their blood. But when Beliardis returns, she finds the children revived, happily playing with red apples. Amicus's leprosy never returns.

Appendix 2.

Vita Amici et Amelii carissimorum.

Summary of KÖLBING, pp.xcvii-cx.

In the days of King Pippin of France, a child is born in Bourges of an illustrious German father. As thanksgiving, the parents vow to God and the blessed apostles Peter and Paul that they will take their child to Rome to be baptised. At the same time, a count in Auvergne has a vision which is explained to him as meaning that his pregnant wife will bear him a son, whom he should have baptised by the Pope. Some two years after the birth of his son he therefore makes his way to Rome; and at Lucca, he meets the German nobleman bringing his own son for baptism. The two infants become very attached to each other; the Pope names the son of the count Amelius, the son of the German nobleman, Amicus. As a christening gift, he gives them two precious cups, both identical in size and design. The fathers then return with their sons to their homeland.

When Amicus is thirty years old, his dying father enjoins him to observe his Christian duties, and reminds him of the link he has with Amelius by virtue of their common baptism and their physical resemblance. After the death of his father, because of the envy of certain jealous people, Amicus and his family are expelled from his patrimony. He then decides to seek Amelius, and ask Hildegard, King Charlemagne's wife, for advice. In the meanwhile, Amelius, hearing of the death of Amicus's father, has set out to visit his friend; he is most disappointed not to find him, and vows never to return to his homeland before he has met Amicus again. He wanders over France and Germany in vain, while Amicus enters in the service of a nobleman. He stays there for a year and a half before continuing his search for Amelius.

The quest of Amelius lasts for two years; then one day, close to Paris, he meets a pilgrim. He asks him if he has seen Amicus; the pilgrim says no; and Amelius gives him a gift asking him to pray for his soul. That evening, the pilgrim meets Amicus, who asks him if he has heard of Amelius; at which the pilgrim asks why he is making fun of him: "You yourself appear to be Amelius, the son of the count of Auvergne, or so you said, when you asked me this very day if I had seen Amicus, a knight from Bourges". Amicus gives the pilgrim alms, and with his companions hastens to Paris after Amelius. Following a misunderstanding, the two heroes prepare to fight each other, but they discover their identity in time, and thank God for their reunion.

They then go to serve Charlemagne at his court; Amicus is made treasurer and Amelius butler. However, Amicus wishes to see his wife again; he therefore leaves the court after warning Amelius against the king's daughter and count Ardericus. After his departure, however, Amelius casts his eye on the king's daughter and seduces her. Ardericus then hints to Amelius that the cause of his friend's departure was that he had stolen money out of the king's treasure; and he offers Amelius his own friendship, which is rejected. Thereupon, Ardericus denounces Amelius to the king, who decides that the matter must be solved by judicial combat. Queen Hildegard accepts to be Amelius's pledge.

In his frantic search for help, Amelius meets Amicus who is on his way back to court. Amicus suggests that they exchange clothes: he will fight instead of Amelius, while Amelius takes his place in his household. However, Amicus forbids Amelius to touch his wife. When night comes, Amelius therefore places a naked sword in the conjugal bed, warning his "wife" not to approach him under pain of death. Amelius, on his side, arrives at court; Ardericus in the meanwhile was slandering the queen, accusing her of having allowed Amelius to seduce her daughter. The king promises Amicus/Amelius the hand of his daughter Belixenda if he wins, and the Queen and her ladies retire to pray for the combatants. Before the battle, Amelius realises that he is about to commit a sin. He tries to avoid the fight by offering his friendship to Ardericus, but Ardericus refuses to withdraw his charge. The fight takes place, Amicus cuts off the head of Ardericus and is given the girl in marriage. He then goes with his young wife to his (Amicus's) house. When Amelius sees his friend coming with an army, he thinks he has been vanquished, and attempts to flee; but he is reassured by Amicus, who takes his rightful place in his household again.

God then afflicts Amicus with leprosy. His wife Obias grows to hate him and tries on several occasions to kill him. Amicus finally asks two faithful servants, Azonis and Horatus, to take him away from his cruel wife. Rejected by all, Amicus decides to go to Rome, to his godfather the Pope, who looks after him for three years. Famine then strikes the city, and Amicus has to leave; he asks his servants to lead him to Amelius. Amelius sends alms of food and wine to the unknown beggar, and his servant reports that the leper has exactly the same cup as his master. Amelius thus recognises Amicus; he takes him in his household.

107

One night, as the two friends are sleeping in the same room in the absence of Amelius's wife, the angel Raphael appears to Amicus, telling him that his prayers have been heard: he must tell Amelius God's instructions, that he must kill his two sons and wash him, Amicus, in their blood. The leprosy will then be cured. Amicus refuses the thought that his friend's children should be killed because of him, but the angel insists that it is God's will. Amelius overhears this conversation and asks Amicus about it. Amicus, after pretending he was just praying aloud, has to tell him about the vision. Amelius reacts badly to the news, but eventually accepts that his friend is telling the truth. Bearing in mind the sacrifice of Abraham he decides to murder his sons. He beheads them, gathers their blood and washes his friend with it. Amicus is instantly cured, and both men praise God. When Amicus's wife comes home, she cannot tell which of the two men is her husband. And when Amelius enters his children's chamber again, he finds them playing in bed, with only a fine red scar around their neck.

Amicus and Amelius then decide to devote their lives to God living in chastity till the end of their days; the wicked wife of Amicus is taken away by a demon and thrown down a cliff, and Amicus is reinstated in his land. The heroes then fight at the side of Charlemagne whilst leading a life of prayer and fasting, and meet with their death on battlefield at Mortaria. The bodies were buried in two different churches, but by the grace of God, the body of Amelius was found with its coffin beside that of Amicus. The account ends with the words: *Explicit vita sanctorum Amici et Amelii.*

Appendix 3.

Ami et Amile, chanson de geste.

Summary of DEMBOWSKI.

The heroes are conceived on the same night and are born on the same day. Ami is the son of the count of Clermont-Ferrand and Amile's father is from Bourges. The parents of the children, told by an angel of the great friendship that will unite the heroes, have them baptized in Rome by the Pope, who gives his two godsons two identical cups. The children resemble each other so much that no one can tell them apart. Ami and Amile then return to their respective homes; when they are fifteen years old, they simultaneously decide to leave their homes to look for each other. After a long quest, which follows the main medieval pilgrimage routes, they meet again, swear to keep an eternal friendship, and go to serve Charlemagne. The treacherous Hardré becomes jealous of the prowess of the heroes; after failing in his attempt to discredit them in the eyes of Charlemagne, he offers Amile the hand of his niece Lubias, the lady of Blaye, as a peace-offering. However, it is Ami who marries the lady; she does her best to make mischief between the two friends.

In the meanwhile, Charlemagne's daughter Belissant, who was favourably disposed towards the heroes from their arrival at court, falls passionately in love with Amile. During an absence of Ami, who has gone to visit his wife and young son, Belissant slips into Amile's bed one night, pretending she is a chamber-maid. Hardré finds them in bed together and denounces them to Charlemagne; Amile, who has to prove his innocence in judicial combat, rides off to Blaye to seek help from his companion. In Blaye, Ami has a bad dream; despite the jealousy of his wife he decides to go to Paris. On his way he comes across Amile, who has fallen asleep in a field. Ami hears of the situation, and decides to take Amile's place in the combat; the friends exchange clothes, and Amile goes to Blaye pretending to be Ami. But at night, much to Lubias's displeasure, he puts his sword between them in bed.

Ami arrives in time to save Amile's guarantors - the queen, Belissant and her brother Bueves. After a long battle, he kills Hardré, who has declared himself a servant of the devil, and Charlemagne gives him the hand of Belissant, insisting that the ceremony take place immediately. Ami's attempts to avoid bigamy fail; despite the warning of an angel that this sin will be punished by leprosy, rather than betray his friend, he allows himself to be betrothed to the girl. Ami and Amile exchange places again; then Ami becomes a leper. Lubias refuses to keep his illness secret; she tries to bribe the bishop to get her marriage annulled. Ami's leprosy becomes public, and he is expelled from his house. He is helped at first by his young son, who however gets thrown into prison when his mother hears of it. Ami is then taken to Rome by two faithful serfs; the Pope looks after him there. But the Pope dies, and Ami decides to return to Clermont. One of his serfs sells himself to mariners to pay for their journey.

They eventually arrive at Riviers, Amile's residence. Thanks to the cup, Amile recognises the leper to be his companion and nurses him. An angel appears to Ami telling him that it is God's will that if Amile washes him in the blood of his sons while Belissant is at mass, he will be cured of his leprosy. Ami tells Amile, who after much soul-searching decides to do as the angel said. In the nursery, Amile's elder son wakes up as his father is about to kill him; he approves of Amile's resolution, promises to pray for him in heaven and presents his neck to be cut. The blood of the children cleanses Ami, whose resemblance to Amile is once again complete. At her return from mass, Belissant cannot tell which is her husband. Amile confesses the murder of their children to her, but when she enters the children's chamber, she finds them playing with a golden apple. A great feast takes place to celebrate the miracle. Ami then decides to go to see his wife Lubias and his son. He first exiles his wife, but quickly reinstates her, and hands over his estate to his son. Ami and Amile then go on pilgrimage to the Sepulchre of Christ, and die on their way back, in Lombardy. Their grave may still be seen, and their story will be remembered till the end of the world.

Appendix 4.

Amys e Amillyoun.

Summary of FUKUI.

Amys and Amillyoun are the sons of two barons; they resemble each other to an astonishing degree. They make a vow of mutual brotherhood and serve their lord with great loyalty. Amys is made butler and Amillyoun marshal at their lord's court. But at the death of his father Amillyoun has to return to his estates. Before leaving court, he warns Amys against becoming friendly with the treacherous seneschal, and enjoins him to remain loyal to his lord. After parting from his friend, Amys meets the seneschal who offers him his friendship and is rebuffed. While Amillyoun gets married in his lands, Amys is noticed at a feast by the count's daughter, named Mirabele but known as Florie. She declares her passion to him; he rejects her advances out of loyalty to his lord; she threatens to tell her father that he has tried to dishonour her, whereupon Amys agrees to meet her secretly. But their conversation is overheard and it is reported to the seneschal, who denounces the lovers to the count on the day following their tryst. Amys has to prove their innocence in judicial combat; the countess acts as his pledge, and he sets out to consult Amillyoun as what to do. Night comes and he falls asleep under a tree. That night, Amillyoun dreams that his friend is in danger. He immediately sets out, and finds Amys under his tree. Amillyoun decides to change places with Amys and tells him to treat his wife as he would himself, to avoid her noticing the substitution. However, at night, Amys places a sword in bed between the two of them. In the meanwhile, Amillyoun arrives at court just in time to prevent the execution of the countess and her daughter. The battle takes place; Amillyoun eventually wins, and is given the girl's hand in marriage. Before entering the church where the wedding is to take place, however, a voice warns the hero that if he marries her, he will be a leper before the three years are out. Rather than betray Amys, Amillyoun goes through with the ceremony. He reveals his real identity to Florie, then he and his companion meet again to exchange their clothes a second time. Amillyoun discovers Amys's chastity, but he does not confide in his wife.

In due time, he becomes a leper; his wife and all his friends reject him, with the exception of the young son of a relative of his. They

111

have to go to live in a hut on the outskirts of the town and suffer great discomfort, but the child, named Uwein but generally called Amorant, refuses to leave him. The child goes to Amillyoun's lady to ask for an ass on which the leper may ride. She gives them one; leper and child then leave the area. But a famine breaks out. In order to eat, they have to sell the ass; Uwein then carries his master around in a wheelbarrow. They eventually arrive at Amys's court where they join the beggars. One of the courtiers is struck by the beauty of the child and offers to take him in service. Uwein refuses; the incident is reported to Amys who decides to send half of each of his dishes to them. The two companions both have identical cups: in serving the wine, the butler notices that the beggar's cup is similar to that of his master, and tells Amys who rushes out to beat the beggar, assuming that his friend's cup has been stolen. When Amys has tired himself out beating him, he asks the beggar where he got his cup from; Amillyoun's answer is a request for a swift death. Uwein reveals the leper's identity, and Amys takes in his friend and nurses him.

One night Amys has a vision: a voice tells him that if he kills his children and bathes Amillyoun in their blood, he will be cured. Amys beheads his sons and their blood cures Amillyoun. Amys's lady thanks God for the cure, and after mass they go to the nursery where they find the children playing in the sun. When Amillyoun is properly recovered, he goes back to his land; his wife was about to remarry that very month. Amillyoun banishes her to a tower where she dies after a year and a day. Amillyoun makes Uwein his heir and ends his life in piety. Both he and his brother are buried in Lombardy where through God's grace their relics accomplish miracles.

Glossary

This glossary contains all the words found in our text (excluding the notes). In the case of variant spellings, the headword is that coming first in alphabetical order, except where this may cause confusion. Entries are structured as follows:

word, variant: part of speech, translation, grammatical description (if relevant), stanza and line of the first three occurrences of the word and its variants; **other forms of word** (e.g. other cases, tenses, etc.): grammatical description, stanza and line of first three occurrences [*etymology*]

Abbreviations:
E. Frisian - Early Frisian, M.Du. - Middle Dutch, M.E. - Middle English, M.L.G. - Middle Low German, O.E. - Old English, O.Fr. - Old French, O.H.G. - Old High German, O.N. - Old Norse, ? - uncertain. If no provenance is given for a word, it is a Middle-English formation.

adj. - adjective, adv. - adverb/adverbial, art. - article, aux. - auxiliary, card. - cardinal, comp. - comparative, conj. - conjunction, constr. - construction, cp. - compare, def. - definite, dem. - demonstrative, esp. - especially, expr. - expression/expressing, fem. - feminine, gen. - genitive, ger. - gerund, imp. - imperative, impers. - impersonal, indef. - indefinite, inf. - infinitive, interj. - interjection, masc. - masculine, nom. - nominative, num. - numeral, obl. - oblique case, obsc. - obscure, ord. - ordinal, orig. - origin, p. - past, part. - participle, pers. - personal, pl. - plural, poss. - possessive, prep. - preposition, pres. - present, pron. - pronoun, refl. - reflexive, rel. - relative, sing. - singular, sb. - substantive, subord. - subordination, subj. - subjunctive, superl. - superlative, v. - verb/verbal, var. - variant, w. - with.

An asterisk following a line reference indicates a difficulty discussed in a footnote. An asterisk before a word indicates a hypothetical form.

a, an: a) indef. art., 6:2,7, etc. [O.E. *ān*]

b) unstressed variant of prep.: See **on**

abbey: sb., abbey 201:2 [O.Fr. *abbeie*]

abed, abedde: adv., in bed, 93:5, 121:11 [O.E. *on bedde*]

abide, abyde: v., stay, wait, remain, stop, inf., imp. and pres., 10:6, 14:3, 34:12, etc. [O.E. *abīdan*]

abode: sb., delay, 80:7 [cp. O.E. *bād*, waiting, and *abīdan*]

aboute: adv. and prep., about, around, close by, 67:1, 84:5, 148:2, etc. [O.E. *on-būtan*]

abye: v., pay for, be punished, inf., 32:6 [O.E. *ābycgan*]

adoun: prep. and adv., down, downwards, 23:12, 78:3, 87:8, etc. [O.E. *ādūne*, from a height]

afefed: v., enfief, endow, p.part., 201:3. [O.Fr. *feffer*]

aferde: v., terrify, p.part., 77:5 [O.E. *āfǣran*]

affys: sb., office, 16:5 [O.Fr. *office*]

afore: prep., before, in front of, 114:5 [O.E. *on foran*]

afote: adv., on foot (i.e. not on horseback), 24:1, 81:2, 110:2, etc. [O.E. *on fōtum*]

after: adv. and prep., after, afterwards, along, following, for (to send, ask, -), 6:5, 27:10, 33:10, etc. [O.E. *æfter*]

afterward: adv., afterwards, then, 123:10 [O.E. *æfterweard*]

agayn, ayan, ayayn, aye, ayen: adv. and prep., again, in return, back (to answer, bring, come/go -), 11:1, 22:12, 28:5, etc. [O.E. *on gēan*]

agon, agoo, agoon: v., go, pass, p.part., 103:10, 176:10, 55:9, etc. [O.E. *āgān*]

agynne: v., begin, start, p., 33:1 [O.E. *onginnan*]

alas: interj., alas, 90:12, 128:1, 136:12, etc. (O.Fr. *(H)a las, hélas*)

all, alle, al: adj. and adv., all, entirely, 1:2, 3:10, 5:5, etc. [O.E. *eall*]

allmost: See **almost**

allmyghti, allmyghty, al-myght: adj., almighty, omnipotent, 102:11, 124:3, 154:4 [O.E. *ealmihtig*]

allso, allsoo, also, alsoo: adv., also, 18:5, 30:6, 48:10, etc. [O.E. *alswā*]

almost, allmost, almoste: adv., almost, very nearly, 21:6, 32:2, 146:4, etc. [O.E. *eall(e) mǣst*]

almyght: See **allmyghti**

alone, alon: adj. and adv., alone, only, unaccompanied, 47:4, 60:2, 85:12, etc. [from phrase *al one*]

als: adv., variant of **also**, in adverbial phrases such as **als swythe**, very quickly, immediately, 172:10; **als tyde, tyde, tyte** (from O.N. *tīðr*, frequent), immediately, as soon as, 46:7, 47:1, 85:1, etc.

alyght: vb., dismount, p.part., 121:1 [O.E. *ālīhtan*]

alyve: adj. and adv., alive, 5:2, 58:6, 61:12, etc. [From expr. *on līve*]

among: adv. and prep., among, in the presence of, in addition,

114

continually, again and again, here and there, 43:11, 50:8, 56:8, etc. [O.E. *on gemong*]

amorn, amorowe: adv., in the morning, 80:1, 82:5, 178:7, etc. [O.E. *on morgen(e)*]

an: See a

and: conj., and, if, 1:6,9,11, etc. [O.E. *and*]

angell, aungell: sb., angel, 125:7, 177:5, 178:2, etc. [O.E. *engel*, from Lat. *angelus*]

anon, anone: adv., immediately, 37:4, 47:1, 51:8, etc.; **anone ryght**: straightaway, 24:4 [O.E. *on ān(e)*]

another: pron., another, 165:8 [O.E. *ān + ōðer*]

anoynted: v., anoint, p., 188:2 [O.Fr. *enoindre*, p.part. *enoint*]

ansuerd, ansuerde, answerd, aunsuerd: v., answer, p., 11:1, 19:2, 22:2, etc.; - **again**: to reply, 38:1. [O.E. *andswarian*]

anyght: adv., at night, 83:2, 93:5, 97:4, etc. [From expr. *on niht*]

aplyght: adv., in faith, indeed (emphatic, esp. in rime), 4:5, 94:1, 120:9, etc. [From *I the aplight*, I assure you]

aquite: v., repay, requite, inf., 161:12, 195:11; **aquitest**: 2 sing. pres., 170:11 [O.Fr. *aquiter*]

arend: sb, message, 155:11 [O.E. *ǣrende*]

armes: sb, (human) arm, pl., 62:8, 119:10, 169:5, etc. [O.E. *earm*]

armour: sb., armour, weapons, 111:5, 112:2 [O.Fr. *armeüre*]

aryght: a) adv., properly, truly, 91:10 [From expr. *on right*]

b) v., approach, inf., 120:6 [O.E. *rihtan*, cp. O.H.G. *arrichtan*]

aryse: v., arise, rise from sleep, imp. and pres., 79:2, 85:4, 87:2 [O.E. *ārīsan*]

as, als: conj., as, like, in the way that, 10:12, 14:12, 41:3, etc.; part of compound conj.: **where as**, where, 2:6; in expr.: **as tyde, as tyte**: immediately; **as tyde as**, as soon as, 46:7, 190:1 [O.E. *eal-swā*, just as]

aske: v., ask, pres., 99:10; **asked**: p., 37:4, 55:7, 120:1, etc. [O.E. *āscian*]

asking: sb., request, 53:2 [O.E. *āscung*]

aslepe: adv., asleep, 82:3, 188:8 [From expr. *on slepe*]

asonder: adv., separately, apart, 119:1, 165:12 [O.E. *on sundran*]

aspye: v., observe, inf., 57:5, 59:11, 182:1. [O.Fr. *espier*]

asse: sb., ass, donkey, sing., 142:9, 143:9, 145:1, etc.; **asses**: pl. 144:2,8, 146:8, etc. [O.E. *assa*]

aston: v., stun, astound, p.part., 105:1 [O.Fr. *estoner*]

asword: v., swear, promise on oath, p., 70:6. [O.E. *āswerian*]

aswoun: adv., in a swoon, 174:10 [cp. O.E. *geswōgen*]

at: prep., at, from, on, 4:9, 13:7, 15:8, etc. [O.E. *æt*]

ateynt: v., convict (of a crime), p.part., 69:9. [O.Fr. *ataindre*]

atwayn, atwynne, atwo, atwoo: adv., in two, into pieces, apart, 23:10, 33:2, 48:11, etc. [O.E. *on twēgen*] aungell, aunsuerd: See angel, ansuerd

auntres: sb., news, event, pl., 179:2. [O.Fr. *aventure*]

avenaunt: adj., gracious, comely, attractive, 35:7, 154:8 [O.Fr. *avenant*]

aventure: sb., adventure, experience, 103:8. [O.Fr. *aventure*]

awake: v., wake up, awaken, inf., 84:1; awaked: p., 193:7 [O.E. *āwacian*]

away, awayn, awey: prep., away, 22:9, 43:12, 47:3, etc.; with aux., go away, disappear, 22:9, 177:12 [O.E. *onweg*]

awe, own: adj., own (emphatic use after poss. noun or pron.), 78:10, 122:11, 128:4, etc. [O.E. *āgen*]

ayan, ayayn, aye: See agayn

ayen: See agayn, ayens

ayens, ayen: prep., against, towards, opposite, with regard to, 25:4, 46:10, 64:2, etc. [O.E. *ongēan*]

bad, bade, bede: v., ask, pray, beg, request, order, offer, p., 26:4, 47:2, 73:8, etc. [O.E. *biddan*]

baded: v., bathe, wash, p., 175:9 [O.E. *baðian*]

bak: sb., back, 108:7 [O.E. *bæc*]

bale: sb., misery, torment, 188:12 [O.E. *bealo*]

bare: adj., bare, naked, deprived, 84:9, 96:11, 111:3, etc. [O.E. *bær*]

baron: sb., baron, sg., 8:2, 38:4, 68:9, etc.; barons, barones, barouns: pl., 1:5,7, 3:4, etc. [O.Fr. *baron*].

basyn: sb., basin, 185:5 [O.Fr. *bacin*]

batell, bataile, bataill, batayle: sb., battle, 68:10, 70:11, 72:9, etc.; don/(under) fongen/leden - to engage in combat, 69:2, 79:10, 90:3, etc. [O.Fr. *bataille*].

bathe: sb., bath, 175:10 [O.E. *bæð*]

be: See ben, by

become: v., become, p., 2:5, 126:6 [O.E. *becuman*]

bed, bedd, bedde: sb, bed, 40:6, 43:3, 83:2, etc. [O.E. *bed*]

bede: a) See bad
b) sb., prayer, 189:11 [O.E. *gebed*]

bedene: adv, at once, all together, 71:9 [orig. obscure]

befall: v., happen, occur, p.part., 126:10, 130:2; befill, befille, befyll: p., 3:2, 29:1, 81:1, etc. [O.E. *befeallan*]

before, beforen, beforn, byforen: adv. and prep., before, beforehand, 25:1, 65:11, 75:3, etc. [O.E. *beforan*].

began: v., begin, p., 140:8,9 [O.E. *beginnan*]

begate: v., beget, engender, p., 124:10 [O.E. *begitan*]

begge: v., beg, inf., 138:11, 142:11; beggyd, p., 145:11 [O.Fr. *begger*, formed to go with sb. *begart*].

begon, bygoon: v., cover, surround, beset, p.part., 83:9, 104:6, 126:3, etc. [O.E. *begān*]

behalde, beholde: v., see, behold, inf., 5:9, 5:11, 7:5; beheld, behelde: p., 8:9, 58:8, 154:7, etc. [O.E. *behealdan*].

behoved: v., need, have to (with dative pers. obj.), pres., 146:8* [O.E. *behōfian*]

behynde: adj., slow in coming, late, 176:8 [O.E. *behindan*]

116

beker: v., fight (mod. Engl. refl., to bicker), inf., 107:2 [cp. E.Frisian *bikkern*, hack].

beknow: v., reveal, subj., 105:7 [O.E. *becnāwan*, acknowledge]

belefte: v., remain, p., 42:5, 181,10, 182:9 [Q.E. *belǣfan*]

bemene: v., lament, pity, subj., 127:9 [O.E. *bimǣnan*]

ben, bene, bien, be, bee: v., be, inf., imp. and pres. subj., 10:8, 16:6, 24:10, etc,; **ben, yben:** p.part., 50:7,9, 65:8, etc.; **am:** 1 sing. pres.; **art, arte, beth:** 2 sing. pres.; **is, ys:** 3 sing. pres., 1:12, 6:9, 29:4, etc.; **are, ben:** pl. pres., 1:2, 91:9, 93:10; **was:** sing. p., 4:8,10,11, etc.; **wes:** sing. and pl. p., 7:11, 41:11, 56:4, etc.; **ware, were, waren,** pl. p. and p.subj., 1:7,11, 2:2, etc. [O.E. *bēon*]

benche: sb., bench, 153:3 [O.E. *benc*]

bende, bonde: sb., captivity, bond, 101:9, 155:9, [O.E. *bend*/ O.N. *band*]

berd, berde: sb., maiden, damsel, sing., 39:2, 46:8, 48:2, etc. [O.E. *brȳd*]

berdes: a) sb., youth, nobleman, pl., 2:3 [O.E. *byrd*, birth, lineage] b) sb., roast meat, dish, pl., 36:6 [O.E. *brǣde*]

bere: v., bear, carry, support, produce, charge (with a crime), inf. and imp., 149:12, 155:11, 162:7; **bare:** pres. and p., 12:5, 25:2, 28:9, etc.; **born, boren, yborn,** p.part., 2:10, 4:5, 48:3, etc. [O.E. *beran*]

beres: sb., bear, pl., 83:7 [O.E. *bera*]

beryed: v., bury, p.part., 192:7 [O.E. *byrigan*]

beset: v., surround, p.part., 83:9* [O.E. *besettan*]

besouche: v., beg, entreat, beseech, pres., 143:7; **besought, besougth:** p., 10:5, 11:8, 21:8, etc. [O.E. *besǣcan*]

best: adv. and adj. (superl.), best, in the best way, 104:8, 105:4, 126:5, etc. [O.E. *betst*]

besteked: v., shut, lock, p.part, 153:11 [cp. M.Du. *besteken*]

bestryde: v., mount, inf., 145:1 [O.E. *bestrīdan*]

bestys: sb., beast, pl., 84:4 [O.Fr. *beste*]

besyde, beside: prep.and adv., at (one's) side, beside, nearby, close to, 45:4, 66:6, 96:6, etc. [O.E. *bīsīdan*]

beteche: v., entrust, commit, pres., 50:11; **betaugh:** p., 27:4 [O.E. *betǣcan*]

bethoght, bethought: v., (refl.), reflect, meditate, p., 42:7, 62:7, 120:7 [O.E. *beðencan*]

better: adv. and adj. (comp.), better, preferable, 29:11, 53:2, 134:6, etc. [O.E. *betera*]

betwene, betuene: prep., between, amid, 12:10, 57:8, 66:8, etc. [O.E. *betwēonan*]

bewrayn: v., accuse, betray, p., 89:10 [From O.E. *wrēgan*]

bey: v., buy, inf., 137:11, 138:5; **boght, bought, ybought,** p.part., 20:6, 42:10, 50:3, etc. [O.E. *bycgan*] beyonde: prep., beyond, on the other side, 1:2 [O.E. *begeondan*]

bien: See ben

blade, (schulder -): sb., (shoulder) blade, 112:8 [O.E. *blæd*]

blak: adj., pale, 197:10 [O.E. *blāc*]

blake: adj., black, dark, 84:4, 199:2 [O.E. *blæc*]

blawe: v., utter, sound, blow, inf., 99:3, 153:2 [O.E. *blāwan*]

ble: sb., complexion, face, 196:11 [O.E. *blēo*]

blessed: v., bless, p., 28:8; yblessed: p.part., 148:12 [O.E. *bletsian*]

blode: sb., blood, living creature, 5:12, 28:8, 32:5, etc. [O.E. *blōd*]

bloo: adj., blue-black, 84:4 [cp. O.Fr. *bleu*, O.N. *blār*]

blynne: v., cease, rest from, inf., 33:4, 180:6 [O.E. *blinnan*]

blysfull: adj., happy, pleasing, blissful, 42:12 [From *blysse*]

blysse: sb., bliss, pleasure, joy, 5:8, 34:12, 84:9, etc. [O.E. *bliss*]

blyssing: sb., blessing, 11:7 [O.E. *bletsung*]

blyth, blythe: adj., happy, joyful, 5:5, 9:6, 14:4, etc. [O.E. *blīðe*]

bode: v., endure, experience, p., 171:12 [O.E. *bīdan*]

body: sb., body, person, sg., 7:7, 38:5, 72:4, etc.; bodyes: pl., 73:9 [O.E. *bodig*]

boght: See bey

boke: sb., book, 37:3 [O.E. *bōc*]

bold, bolde: adj., bold, strong, noble, 2:3, 7:2, 9:2, etc. [O.E. *beald*].

bonde: a) sb., servant, retainer, 6:5, 200:2 [O.E. *bonda*]

b) See bende

bone: sb., bone, 5:12, 12:10, 28:8, etc.; bones, bonys: pl., 96:10, 170:9 [O.E. *bān*]

borde: sb., dining table, 129:8, 167:1 [O.E. *bord*]

boren, born: See bere

borow, borowe: sb., pledge, surety, sing., 73:3, 90:6, 71:1; borowes, borows, pl., 71:8, 73:11, 74:2, etc. [From v. *borwen* (O.E. *borgian*), guarantee]

bosked: See busked

boste: sb., boast, noise, 99:3 [cp. O.Fr. *bost*]

bote: a) v., cure, make better, inf., 188:12 [O.E. *bōtian*]

b) sb., remedy, redress, 192:8 [O.E. *bōt*]

bote: See both, but

boteler, botelere: sb., butler, chief servant in charge of drink, 16:8, 36:7, 38:7, etc. [O.Fr. *boteillier*]

both, bothe, bote: adj. and pron., both, 2:9, 4:4, 5:3, etc. [O.E. phrase *bā ðā*; cp. O.N. *bāðir*]

bought: See bey, bowgh

boun: v., go, proceed, inf., 23:3* [From adj. *boun*; cp. O.N. *būin*]

bounte: sb., bounty, goodness, 1:5, 16:3 [O.Fr. *bonté*].

bour, boure: sb., bower, (lady's) chamber, 6:6, 27:10, 35:10, etc. [O.E. *būr*]

bourde: sb., joke, anecdote, 157:11 [O.Fr. *bourde*]

bowe: sb., bow (for shooting), 42:2 [O.E. *boga*]

bowgh, bought: sb., bough, branch, 42:10, 45:5 [O.E. *bōg*]

brake: See breke

118

brayd, braide, brayde: v., draw (a sword), move quickly, p., 87:4, 95:11, 167:3 [O.E. *bregdan*]

brayn: sb., brain, 109:6 [O.E. *brægen*]

bredale: sb., wedding-feast, 197:3, 198:12 [O.E. *brȳd-ealo*]

brede: sb., bread, 137:11, 138:6, 146:5, etc. [O.E. *brēad*, crumb]

breke: v., break, inf., 21:1, 30:11, 31:8, etc.; brekest: 2 sing. pres., 170:9; brake, broke: p., 39:8, 127:2 [O.E. *brecan*]

breng, brenge, bring, bryng: v., bring, inf., 17:5, 28:12, 57:12, etc.; brynge: imp., 162:12; brought, brouth: p. and p.part., 27:11, 55:10, 58:11, etc. [O.E. *brengan*].

brenne: v., burn, inf., 100:6; brent: p.part., 99:11 [O.N. *brenna*/ O.E. *biernan*]

breste: sb., breast, chest, 112:7 [O.E. *brēost*]

broder: See brother

brond, bronde: sb., sword, blade, sg., 91:11, 168:6; brondes: pl., 111:3, 198:5 [O.E. *brand*]

brother, broder: sb., brother, sg., 20:2, 21:11, 22:10, etc.; brothers: pl., 166:4 [O.E. *brōðor*]

brotherede: v., become sworn brothers, p.part, 30:2* [From *brother*].

broune: adj., brown, (of weapons) bright, 15:3, 198:5, 199:2 [O.E. *brūn*]

brouth: See breng

bryght: adj., bright, beautiful, 6:6, 7:7, 27:10, etc. [O.E. *beorht*].

busked, bosked: v., get ready, prepare, p., 23:5, 41:6, 85:5, etc. [O.N., *būask*]

but: adv., conj. and prep., outside, without, except, unless, but, 25:10, 26:11, 47:10, etc. [O.E. *būtan*]

by, be: prep, by, at, during, 14:6, 67:4, 104:2, etc. [O.E. *bi*]

byde: v., stay, live, remain, inf., 152:12 [O.E. *bīdan*]

byforen: See beforen

bygoon: See begon

byhight: v., promise, p., 81:6 [O.E. *behātan*]

call: v., call, inf., 130:1; callid: p.part., 4:8,10. [O.E. *ceallian*/ O.N. *kalla*]

cam, came: See come

can: v. (modal aux.), know, can, pres., 65:5, 12, 77:12, etc.; coude, couth, cowde, cowth: p., 8:10, 45:8, 54:11, etc. [O.E. *cunnan*]

candell: sb., candle, 182:10 [O.E. *candel*, from Latin *candela*]

care, kare: sb., care, sorrow, 11:9, 21:4, 28:12, etc. [O.E. *caru*]

carefull, carfull, karfull: adj., sad, anxious, sorrowful, 18:7, 81:3, 128:12, etc. [O.E. *carful*]

cas: sb., incident, event, case, 89:7, 126:10, 175:5 [O.Fr. *cas*]

caste, kaste: vb., cast, throw, p., 65:11, 57:2, 154:5, etc. [O.N. *kasta*]

castell: sb., castle, 152:7, 162:7, 163:2, etc. [O.E., from O.Fr. *castel*]

catell: sb., property, income, 149:7 [O.Fr. *catel*, from Latin *capitale*]

caughte: v., catch, seize, p., 198:8*
[O.Fr. *chacier*]

certenly: adv., certainly, absolutely,
137:10 [From O.Fr. *certain*]

certes, certeys: adv., certainly,
22:6, 25:12, 29:6, etc. [O.Fr.
certes]

chamber: sb., chamber, 54:10,
59:5,8, etc. [O.Fr. *chambre*]

chanoun: sb., canon, clergyman
living under canon rule, 50:4 [O.Fr.
chanoine]

chapell: sb., chapel, 189:2 [O.Fr.
chapelle]

charyte: sb., charity, Christian
love, 21:9*, 130:12, 172:7* [O.Fr.
charité]

chased: v., chase away, p., 128:9
[O.Fr. *chacier*]

chaunge: v., change, inf., 48:8;
chaunged: p. and p.part., 49:2,
96:9 [O.Fr. *changier*]

chefe, chief: sb., chief, head, 17:2,
16:8 [O.Fr. *chief*]

cheping: sb., market, 138:8,
139:6,7, etc. [O.E. *cīeping*]

chere: sb., countenance, expression,
face, 2:3, 14:4, 43:4, etc. [O.Fr.
chiere]

chese: See chose

child, childe: sb., youth, child
(used before or after a name,
indicates an aspirant to
knighthood), 4:11, 12:2, 132:4,
etc.; childer, childerin,
childern, childeryn: pl., 1:10,
2:9,11, etc. [O.E. *cild*]

childe: v., protect, shield, inf., 11:9
[O.E. *scieldan*]

chirche: sb., church, 4:9, 152:5,
180:10, etc. [O.E. *cirice*]

chonge: v., change, inf., 31:12;
chonged, chongyd: p., 92:8,
118:5 [O.Fr. *changier*]

chose, chese: v., choose, inf.,
26:5, 164:5; chosen: p.part.,
38:12 [O.E. *cēosan*]

cite: sb., city, 148:9 [O.Fr. *cité*]

clay: sb., earth, clay, 40:12 [O.E.
clæg]

cleped, clepid: v., call, name, p.,
10:3, 162:2 [O.E. *clipian*]

clere: adj., clear, 69:3 [O.Fr. *cler*]

cloddes: sb., lump of earth, clot,
pl., 124:6 [O.E. *clott*]

cloth: sb., clothing, clothes, sing.,
8:12, 137:3; clothes: pl., 51:7,
175:11, 188:6 [O.E. *clāð*]

cold, colde: sb. and adj., cold,
124:6, 135:8, 153:12 [O.E. *ceald*]

colowr: sb., colour, 8:12 [O.Fr.
colour]

comaunded: v., command, order;
p., 100:2, 144:8, 158:1 [O.Fr.
comander]

come: v., come, inf., 134:5,
143:11, 144:11, etc.; comest: 2
sing. pres., 79:7; cometh: 3 sing.
pres., 100:11; cam, came, come:
p.,7:3, 18:2, 23:3, etc.; come,
ycome, ycomen: p.part., 4:12,
22:8, 48:3, etc. [O.E. *cuman*]

comely: adj., noble, splendid, 10:2,
19:1, 22:1 [O.E. *cȳmlic*]

comyng: sb., arrival, 55:2, 117:8
[From ger. of v. *come*]

conforted: v., comfort, p., 192:3,
193:2 [O.Fr. *conforter*]

contray, contraye, contre,
contrey, cuntre, cuntrey: sb.,
region, country, 2:10, 11:12,
22:10, etc. [O.Fr. *contree*]

coppe, couppe, couppes: See cuppe

corn: sb., corn, grain, 140:8 [O.E. *corn*]

coude: See can

councell, counseyll: sb., advice, counsel, 63,3,12, 64:3 [O.Fr. *conseil*]

court, courte: sb., court, 2:6, 7:3, 8:1, etc. [O.Fr. *cort*]

couth, cowde, cowth: See can

craftes: sb., skill, art, craft, pl., 9:9 [O.E. *cræft*]

crie: sb., in phrase at crie, at call, subject to call, 17:3 [O.Fr. *cri*]

crod, crouded: v., push, p., 150:1, 151:8,11 [O.E. *crūdan*]

croudwayne: sb., push-cart, wheelbarrow, 149:10 [From *crouden*, push, and *wain* (O.E. *wægn*), waggon]

croun: sb., crown, clerical tonsure, 25:2, 50:2 [O.Fr. *corone*]

crystendome: sb., baptism, 159:8 [O.E. *cristendōm*]

crystenyng: sb., christening, baptism, 4:9 [From ger. of v.; cp. O.E. *cristnung*]

cuntre, cuntrey: See contray

cuppe, coppe, couppe: sb., cup, sing., 26:10, 131:9, 146:10, etc.; cuppes, cuppis, cuppys: pl., 20:5, 26:2, 164:1, etc. [O.E. *cuppe*]

curteys: adj., courteous, 5:3 [O.Fr. *corteis*]

dai: See day

dame: sb., (used as title) Madam, lady, 78:4, 130:8, 174:1 [O.Fr. *dame*]

dampne: v., to condemn, pl. imp. (polite form), 68:6; dampneth: imp. (familiar form), 72:10 [O.Fr. *damner*]

dare: v., to dare, to need (in confusion of meaning and form with v. *thurfen*), pres., 72:8, 163:6; darest, dare: 2 sing. pres., 69:2, 76:11; dorst, durst, durste: p., 39:6, 78:7, 90:6, etc. [O.E. *durran*]

day, dai: sb., day, sg., 4:5, 6:11, 9:10, etc.; dayes: pl., 48:4, 58:3, 148:3, etc. [O.E. *dæg*]

dede: a) sb., deed, 3:9, 12:9, 13:8, etc. [O.E. *dǣd*]
b) adj., dead, 18:11, 80:10, 109:7, etc. [O.E. *dēad*]
c) See don.

dedely: adj., mortal, deadly, 180:3 [O.E. *dēaðlic*]

delay: sb., delay, 22:3, 32:3, 47:6, etc. [O.Fr. *délai*]

dele: v., distribute, share out, inf., 137:3 [O.E. *dǣlan*]

demyd: v., condemn, judge, p.part., 51:12 [O.E. *dēman*]

dent: sb., blow, sg., 66:10, 108:8, 109:3, etc.; dentes: pl., 108:5 [O.E. *dynt*]

dere: adj. and adv., dear, dearly, expensive, 14:5, 43:2, 50:3, etc. [O.E. *dēore*]

deth: sb., death, 48:11, 199:10 [O.E. *dēað*]

devell: sb., devil, 50:11 [O.E. *dēofol*, from Latin *diabolus*]

dight: See dyght

discure: v., reveal, inf., 63:12 [O.Fr. *descovrir*]

do: See don

dobbed, dobbid, dubbed: v., arrange, adorn, dub (knight), p. and p.part., 2:7, 14:8, 139:5 [O.E. *dubbian*, O.Fr. *adober*]

does: sb., dais, 56:2 [O.Fr. *deis*, table]

dole: sb., sorrow, 151:12, [O.Fr. *doel*]

doloure: sb., pain, grief, 1:12 [O.Fr. *dolour*]

don, do, doo: v., do, cause (followed by infinitive: passive sense), inf., imp. and subj., 17:11, 25:5, 30:1, etc.; **dost:** 2 sing. pres., 87:10, 187:3; **doth:** imp., 72:6 (= put); **did, dede, dide, dyde:** p., 18:9, 118:6, 126:9, etc.; **don, do, ydo, ydon:** p.part. 65:2, 67:7, 68:5, etc. [O.E. *dōn*]

dore: sb., door, 66:8,11, 186:2 [O.E. *duru*]

dorst: See **dare**

doughter, doghter: sb., daughter, 35:2, 43:2,7, etc. [O.E. *dohtor*]

doughty, douti, dowthi, dowty: adj., doughty, strong, brave, 3:9, 6:2, 15:10, 17:3, 23:2, etc.; **doughtyest:** superl., 15:10, 37:12, 38:10 [O.E. *dyhtig*]

doun: adv., down, 80:10, 95:1, 109:7, etc. [O.E. *dune*]

drawe: v., to draw, to drag, inf., 47:3; **drawe, drawen:** p.part., 52:9, 75:8, 99:9, etc.; **drew, drewe, drowe:** p., 107:10, 152:9, 163:7, etc. [O.E. *dragan*]

drede: a) sb., dread, terror, 66:9, 105:10
b) v., fear, imp. and inf., 76:7,11 [O.E. *drǣdan*]

dreme: sb., dream, vision, 83:3 [O.E. *drēam*]

drere, drery: adj., sorrowful, dejected, 21:7*, 133:12, 185:2 [O.E. *drēorig*, blood-stained, cruel]

drew, drewe: See **dryve**

drink, drinke, drynk, drynke: a) sb., drink, 34:4, 135:11, 139:11, etc.
b) v., drink, inf. and imp., 162:11, 163:6 [O.E. *drincan*]

dryve: v., drive, inf., 61:5; **dreve, drove, dryve, dryven:** p.part., 125:5, 170:4, 174:6, etc. [O.E. *drīfan*]

dubbed: See **dobbed**

duellyng: See **dwellyng**

duke: sb., duke, 6:2, 9:1, 10:2, etc.; **dukes:** gen., 43:2, 63:9, 150:8 [O.Fr. *duc*]

durst, durste: See **dare**

dwelled: v., dwell, remain, p., 97:2, 140:2, 148:3 [O.E. *dwellan*, hinder]

dwellyng, duellyng: sb., delay, 26:6, 55:1, 147:6, etc. [From ger. of v. *dwell*]

dyed, dyde: v., die, p., 32:4, 49:4, 67:4, etc. [O.N. *deyja*]

dyght, dight: v., direct, arrange, prepare, inf., 16:11, 80:1, 85:3, etc. [O.E. *dihtan*]

eche: adj., each, 85:4 [O.E. *ǣlc*]

echon, echone: pron., each one, all, 51:7, 73:10, 85:9, etc. [O.E. *ǣlc ān*]

egre: adj., angry, 63:10, 66:1,12, etc. [O.Fr. *egre*]

eire: sb., heir, 49:6 [O.Fr. *heir*]

eke: adv., equally, also, 47:9 [O.E. *ēac*]

eldres: sb., ancestors, 201:6 [O.E. *ealdor*]

els: adv., else, otherwise, 110:2 [O.E. *elles*]

emperour: sb., emperor, 49:9 [O.Fr. *empereor*]

ende: sb., end, extremity, border, 25:6, 123:9, 126:1, etc. [O.E. *ende*]

enemy: sb., hostility, hatred, 17:9* [O.Fr. *enemi*]

envy: sb., envy, 88:7 [O.Fr. *envie*]

eny: adj., any, 102:6 [O.E. *ænig*]

er, ere: adv., conj. and prep., before, formerly, 7:12, 125:5, 174:9, etc.; er(e) than: prior to that, before the time that, 52:6, 62:12, 75:2, etc. [O.E. *ær*]

erle: sb., earl, generic sing., 8:2, 38:4, 123:5, etc.; erles, erls: pl., 34:8, 9:2 [O.E. *eorl*]

erly: adv., early, 138:1, 147:3 [O.E. *ærlīce*]

erth: sb., earth, ground, 109:5 [O.E. *eorðe*]

erthly: adv., terrestrial, 5:9* [O.E. *eorðlic*]

eten: v., to eat, inf. and p.part., 128:10, 129:2 [O.E. *etan*]

evell: adj. and adv., wicked, evil, badly, 58:12, 122:6, 137:8, etc.; worse, comp., 104:6; worst, superl., 126:8 [O.E. *yfel*]

ever: adv., always, ever, 17:4, 17:11, 20:2, etc.; ever moo, evermore: evermore, always: 10:11, 13:10, 24:7, etc. [O.E. *æfre*]

every: adj., every, 5:8, 13:7, 34:6, etc. [From O.E *æfre* + *ælc*]

everychon, everychone: pron., every one, 37:5, 47:2, 55:12, etc. [From *every* and *on*]

fachon, fauchon: sb., falchion (a short, broad sword, shaped like a sickle), sg., 66:4,11, 112:4; fachons: pl., 108:2 [O.Fr. *fauchon*]

fader: sb., father, 18:5,10, 40:7, etc.; faders: pl. and gen. sing., 1:7, 27:9 [O.E. *fæder*]

faile: a) sb., lack, failure, 68:11, 70:10, 77:7, etc. [O.Fr. *faille*] b) v., fail, inf. and subj., 13:11, 24:8, 91:7; failed: p., 66:6, 109:4 [O.Fr. *faillir*]

faint: sb., weakness, 146:4 [From O.Fr. adj. *faint*]

faire, fayre, ffayre: adj. and adv., fair, pleasant, fairly, 5:12, 7:2, 23:11, etc.; fayrer, ffayrer: comp., 5:2, 7:11, 8:10, etc.; fairest, fayrest: superl., 37:7, 38:5, 159:7 [O.E. *fæger*]

fairehed: sb., beauty, 154:12 [From adj. *faire*]

fale: adj., many, 152:10, 198:3 [O.E. *fela*]

fall: v., fall, imp., 188:8; falle: p.part, 110:6 [O.E. *feallan*]

falle: adj., good, estimable, 36:3, 188:6 [O.E. *fæle*]

fals: adj., false, lying, treacherous, 25:11, 69:8, 106:4 [O.E. *fals*, from Latin *falsum*]

falshede: sb., falsehood, lie, disloyalty: 77:9, 110:12 [From adj. *fals*]

fame: sb., death, disrepute, 105:8 [O.Fr. *fame*]

fare: v., travel, go, fare, inf. and subj., 9:11, 21:2,10, etc.; fare, fere: p., 11:12, 108:3; faren: p.part., 120:2; farest: 2 sing. pres., 96:4, 170:12 [O.E. *faran*]

fare: sb., fortune, course, life, 42:12, 57:6, 95:5, etc. [O.E. *faru*]

fast, faste, ffaste: adv., fast, firmly, quickly, 57:5, 69:7, 182:1, etc. [O.E. *fæste*]

fauchon: See **fachon**

fay: sb., faith, 165:5 [O.Fr. *fei*]

fayn, ffayn: adj. and adv., pleased, gladly, 11:4, 61:2,10, etc. [O.E. *fægen*]

fayre, fayrer, fayrest: See **faire**

feche, fette: v., fetch, seek, inf., 70:4, 133:9, 134:2, etc. [O.E. *feccan*]

fede: v., feed, nourish, pres., 129:8; **fed:** p.part, 199:8 [O.E. *fēdan*]

fee: sb., money, riches, 49:12, 160:7 [O.E. *feoh*]

felawe: sb., friend, companion, 87:2 [O.N. *fēlagi*]

feld: sb., field, 100:7 [O.E. *feld*]

fell, felle: adj., cruel, fierce, 32:1, 59:7, 88:7, etc. [O.E. (*wæl-*)*fel*, greedy for corpses]

felon: sb., traitor, felon, 78:12, 89:2 [O.Fr. *felon*]

felony, felonye: sb., treachery, felony, 17:12, 57:4 [O.Fr. *felonie*]

fen: sb., mud, dirt, 151:11 [O.E. *fenn*]

ferdly, ferly: adj., marvellous, wonderful, terrifying, 46:5, 58:8, 191:12 [O.E. *færlīc*; forms with *d* due to analogy with sb. *ferd*]

fere, ffere: sb., companionship, company, in expr. **in fere**, together, 2:9, 12:3, 33:7, etc. [O.E. (*ge*)*fēra*]

fere: adj., strong, healthy, 109:1, 195:1 [O.E. *fēre*]

fere: a) sb., fire, 100:4, 108:6 [O.E. *fȳr*]
b) sb., fear, 109:9 [O.E. *fyrhto*]

fere: See **fare**

ferly: a) adv., exceedingly, 20:1, 192:1 [O.E. *fērlīce*]
b) See **ferdly**

fest, feste: sb., feast, 6:7, 9:1, 34:2, etc. [O.Fr. *feste*]

fette: See **feche**

ff- : See **f-**

fight, fyght: v., fight, inf. and p., 73:6, 76:8, 77:5, etc.; **fyghtyng:** ger., 108:11 [O.E. *feohtan*]

fill: sb., satiety, fill (of food), 146:5 [O.E. *fyllo*]

fill, fille: See **fyll**

find: v., find, procure, maintain, inf., 10:11; **fond, fonde, founde:** p., 14:10, 15:2, 60:2, etc.; **found, yfounde:** p.part., 31:2, 115:7 [O.E. *findan*]

firste, ffyrst: adv., first, 33:1, 164:2 [O.E. *fyrst*]

fle, flee, flene: v., flee, inf. and subj., 71:12*, 72:7, 105:5, etc. [O.E. *flēon*]

flesche: sb., flesh, 12:10 [O.E. *flæsc*]

floure: sb., flower, the best of, 38:12 [O.Fr. *flour*]

flynte: sb., flint, stone, rock, 109:1 [O.E. *flint*]

fode, food, foode: sb., a) food, 133:9, 139:9
b) offspring, person, 5:9, 46:5, 58:8, etc. [O.E. *fōda*]

fole: sb., fool, madman, 159:10 [O.Fr. *fol*]

folk: sb., people, folk, 6:10, 34:7, 85:4, etc. [O.E. *folc*]

folow: v., follow, inf., 86:6 [O.E. *folgian*]

foly: sb., folly, 160:2* [O.Fr. *folie*]

foman, sb., enemy, foe, 32:8, 76:8 [O.E. *fāhmann*]

fon, foo: sb., enemy, foe, 73:6, 83:6, 104:9, etc. [O.E. *gefā*, from adj. *fāh*]

fonde, fonden: a) See **find**
b) v., seek, hurry, take care, concern or busy oneself with, inf., 13:6, 45:11, 60:2, etc. [O.E. *fandian*]

fonge: v., undertake, seize, inf., 90:3; **fong:** p., 169:5 [O.E. *fōn*]

foo: See **fon**

food, foode: See **fode**

for, ffor: conj. and prep., for, because of, out of, 1:1, 6:4,8, etc.; + inf: in order to, 3:5, 9:9, 10:8, etc.; **for that:** because, 45:9 [O.E. *for*]

forbede: v., forbid, inf. and pres., 25:10, 86:4 [O.E. *forbēodan*]

forest: sb., wood, forest, 81:8, 86:9, 117:9 [O.Fr. *forest*]

forfare: v., destroy, inf., 92:12 [O.E. *forfaran*]

forgon: v., lose, inf., 52:11; p.part., exhausted 86:10 [O.E. *forgān*]

forlayn, forleyn: v., seduce, p.part., 61:5, 64:12, 65:9, etc. [O.E. *forlicgan*]

forlore, forloren, forlorn: v., lose, dishonour, destroy, ruin, p.part, 25:5, 31:8, 48:6, etc. [O.E. *forlēosan*]

fornsworn, forswore, forsworn: v., swear a falsehood, commit perjury, p.part. used as adj.

("forsworn"), 25:4, 31:7, 48:12, etc. [O.E. *forswerian*]

forsake: v., forsake, abandon, deny, inf., 60:10, 69:12, 104:12, etc. [O.E. *forsacan*]

forsayn: v., deny, inf., 65:12 [O.E. *forsecgan*]

forsoth, fforsoth, forsothe: adv. expr., truly, in truth, 4:6, 8:6, 65:10, etc. [O.E. *forsōð*]

fortenyght, fourtenyght, fourthenyght: sb., period of fourteen days, fortnight, 36:1, 71:2, 120:3 [From early M.E. phrase]

forth: adv., forth, forward, 81:5, 100:3, 116:12, etc. [O.E. *forð*]

forthryght: adv., immediately, straightaway, 138:4 [O.E. *forðrihte*]

forward: adv., forth, henceforth, 13:10, 24:7 [O.E. *forðweard*]

foryate: v., forget, p., 97:4 [O.E. *forgietan*]

foryefe: v., forgive, imp., 172:8; **forgafe:** p., 172:10 [O.E. *forgiefan*]

fote: sb., foot, sing., 168:4; **fete:** pl., 139:1, 168:7 [O.E. *fōt*]

foule: adj., foul, dirty, repulsive, 67:8, 129:9, 157:4, etc.; **fouler, ffouler:** comp., 103:11, 125:8 [O.E. *fūl*]

foulehed: sb., impurity, foulness, 193:8 [From adj. *foul*]

foules: sb., bird, pl., 43:10 [O.E. *fugel*]

ffoure: card. num., four, 58:3; **fourth:** ord. num., fourth, 140:7 [O.E. *fēower*]

fra: See **fro**

frayn, frayne: v., ask, question, enquire, inf., 136:4, 160:4 [O.E. *gefrægnan*]

125

fre, free: a) adj., noble, generous, 3:5*, 6:5, 10:7, etc.
b) sb., nobleman, 21:6, 29:3, 179:3 [O.E. frēo]
frend, frende: sb., friend, sing., 2:5, 10:5, 17:8, etc.; frendes, frends: pl., 31:10, 116:4, 119:5 [O.E. frēond]
frendeles: adj., friendless, 126:11 [O.E. frēondlēas]
frere: sb., friar, 50:9 [O.Fr. frere]
fro, fra, froo, ffro: prep. and adv., from, 11:9, 13:10, 18:4, etc. [O.E. fram, O.N. fram, frā]
full, ffull: a) adj., full, 54:2, 57:4, 65:1, etc.
b) adv., very, entirely, thoroughly, 3:12, 7:3, 9:10, etc. [O.E. full]
further: adv., further, 81:12, 139:2 [O.E. fur ðor]
fyght: a) See fight
b) sb., fight, battle, 72:5, 90:2, 169:12 [O.E. feoht]
fyghtyng: See fight
fyll, fill, fille: v., fall, befall, happen, p., 1:2, 80:10, 82:3, etc. [O.E. feallan]
fynd, find, fynde: v., find, inf. and pres., 10:11, 40:4, 62:5, etc.; fond, fonde, founde: p., 14:10, 15:2, 60:2, etc.; found, ffound: p.part, 31:2, 74:2 [O.E. findan]
fyne, ffyne: adj., fine, noble, splendid, 165:8, 190:3 [O.Fr. fin]
fyve, ffyve, five: card. num., five, 5:4, 58:3, 61:9, etc. [O.E. fīf]

galows: sb., gallows, 72:12 [O.E. gealga]

game: sb., game, amusement, mirth, 9:7, 58:2, 117:11, etc. [O.E. gamen]
gan, gon, gone: v., begin, go (often meaningless v. aux. that can be rendered with "do" or "did"), p., 2:1, 5:1, 7:5, etc.; gonne: p.part., 2:1; wenst: 2 sing. p., 88:4; went, wente, p. and p.part., 11:11. 15:7, 20:4, etc. [O.E. gān]
gan: v., help, p., 173:12* [O.N., cp. O.N. gegna]
gardeyn, gardyne: sb., garden, 42:8, 43:8 [O.Fr. gardin]
gate: a) See gete
b) sb., gate, 131:5, 152:7, 153:11, etc. [O.E. geat]
gay: adj., elegant, pleasant, 98:5, 102:9 [O.Fr. gai]
gente: adj., noble, well-born, 143:2 [O.Fr. gent]
gentell, gentil, gentill, gentyl, gentyll, jentyll: adj., noble, well-born, 24:2, 30:8, 35:7, etc.; gentyler: comp., 159:5 [O.Fr. gentil]
gerison: sb., protection, garrison, 198:2 [O.Fr. garison]
geste: sb., guest, 34:5 [O.E. giest]
geste, jeste: sb., poem, "chanson de geste", 3:3, 12:12, 14:1, etc. [O.Fr. geste]
gete: v., get, find, procure, take care of, inf. and subj., 31:10, 139:9, 147:12, etc.; gate: p., 15:12, 28:9, 139:11, etc.; goten, yoten: p.part., begotten, 3:8, 4:4, 163:8 [O.N. geta, O.E. gietan]
geve: v., give, inf., 140:11; yef: imp. and pres., 21:10, 32:11; yafe, yave: p., 11:7, 116:7; yeve: subj., 28:3, 144:11, 184:11 [O.E. giefan]

126

glad: adj., cheerful, glad, 11:4, 14:4, etc. [O.E. *glæd*]

glade, glad: v., gladden, comfort, inf., 9:6, 133:7 [O.E. *gladian*]

gladly: adv., gladly, kindly, 73:2 [O.E. *glædlīce*]

glee: sb., entertainment, music, 44:12 [O.E. *glīw*]

glove: sb., glove, 69:5 [O.E. *glōf*]

glyde, v., rush, inf., 59:10 [O.E. *glīdan*]

go, gon, gone, goo, goon: v., go, inf. and subj., 10:9, 14:6, 30:10, etc.; goth: pres., 137:12; yede, yode, yeden: p., 19:6, 75:2, 99:4, etc.; gon, go, ygo, ywent: p.part., 37:1, 93:7, 126:1, etc. [O.E. *gān*]

gode, good, guode: a) sb., property, good thing, 46:6, 61:8, 67:5, etc.
b) adj., good, 2:4, 5:3, 10:4, etc. [O.E. *gōd*]

gold, golde: a) adj., golden, of gold, 20:5, 131:9
b) sb., gold, 26:2, 146:10, 153:9, etc. [O.E. *gold*]

goldsmyth: sb., goldsmith, 20:4 [O.E. *goldsmiδ*]

goten: See gete

grace: sb., grace, 18:6, 124:2, 150:12, etc. [O.Fr. *grace*]

grame: a) sb., anger, harm, 53:9, 65:1, 89:6, etc. [O.E. *grama*]
b) adj., angry, fierce, 17:10 [O.E. *gram*]

graunt, graunte: v., grant, permit, allow, consent, inf., pres. and subj., 51:4, 52:4, 53:2, etc.; graunted: p., 54:7, 73:12, 74:3, etc. [O.Fr. *granter*]

grave: sb., grave, tomb, 201:8 [O.E. *græf*]

graved: v., bury, p.part., 124:6 [O.E. *grafan*]

grefe: sb., distress, grief, 64:8 [O.Fr. *grief*]

gremely, grymely: adj., fierce, cruel, 108:8, 111:8, 114:9, etc. [O.E. *grimlīc*]

grete: a) adj., great, large, 1:5,6,8, etc. [O.E. *grēat*]
b) v., greet, inf., 46:12 [O.E. *grētan*]

greved: v., grieve, afflict, injure, p. and p.part., 57:9, 111:9 [O.Fr. *grever*]

ground, grounde: sb., ground, earth, 109:7, 171:10, 174:10 [O.E. *grund*]

gryll, grylle: a) sb., suffering, harm, 53:9
b) adj., stern, harsh, 105:3, 146:2 [cp. O.E. *grillan*]

guodehede: sb., goodness, virtue, 201:10 [From adj. *good*]

gyle: sb., trick, guile, treachery, 17:6, 33:11, 57:11, etc. [O.Fr. *guile*]

gyled: v., deceive, betray, p.part., 166:9 [O.Fr. *guiler*]

gylt: sb., guilt, fault, 172:8 [O.E. *gylt*]

gyltles: adj., guiltless, innocent, 75:5, 92:5 [From *gylt*]

habergon: sb., habergeon (piece of mail or scale armour to defend neck and breast), 198:4 [O.Fr. *hauberjon*]

hailed: v., hail, greet, p., 29:3 [From adj. and interj. *heil*; cp. O.N. *heilla*] halde: See hold

halfe: adj., half, 82:11, 129:1, 131:5, etc. [O.E. *healf*]

hall, halle: sb., hall, court, 16:10, 55:3,10, etc. [O.E. *heall*]

halp: See help

han: See have

hard, harde: adj. and adv., hard, 47:8, 51:6, 105:3, etc. [O.E. *heard*]

hardy: adj., bold, brave, 86:5, 196:2 [O.Fr. *hardi*]

hare: adj., dark, old, 42:3 [O.E. *hār*]

harme: sb., harm, injury, affliction, 64:5 [O.E. *hearm*]

harte: See herte

hastelye: adv., hastily, 196:1 [From O.Fr. sb. *haste*]

have, han: v. and aux., have, inf., imp. and 1 sing. pres., 29:7, 31:2, 50:7, etc.; hast: 2 sing. pres., 51:10, 64:7, 93:7, etc.; hath, pres., 38:8, 49:12, 51:1, etc.; had, hadde: p. and subj., 3:5, 5:8, 17:1, etc. [O.E. *habban*]

hayle: adj., healthy, hale, 179:12 [O.N. *heill*]

he: pers. pron., 3 sing. masc. nom.,4:8,11, 6:4, etc.; him, hym: 3 sing. masc. obl., 9:2, 10:3,6, etc.; his, hes: 3 sing. masc. and neuter, poss., 4:9, 6:4, 9:1, etc.; sche, she: 3 sing. fem. nom., 35:4,7,11, etc.; her, here, hire: 3 sing. fem. obl. and poss., 1:7, 27:11, 33:1, etc.; hyt, it, yt: 3 sing. neuter, 1:12, 29:1, 31:9, etc.; thei: 3 pl. nom., 1:11, 2:1,2; him, hem, them: 3 pl. obl. 5:5,8, 7:5, etc.; her, here, ther, there: 3 pl. poss., 3:12, 5:5, 7:2, etc.; him/hem self: refl., 15:12, 23:5, 41:6, etc. [O.E.]

hed, hede, sb., head, 66:9, 112:11, 113:5, etc. [O.E. *hēafod*]

heled: v., heal, cure, p., 115:9 [O.E. *hǣlan*]

hell: sb., hell, 50:11 [O.E. *hell*]

helm, helme: sb., helm, helmet, 102:8, 198:4; helmes: pl., 108:4 [O.E. *helm*]

help, helpe: v., help, succour, inf. and subj., 24:9, 40:9, 78:11, etc.; helpith: 3 sing. pres., 51:2; halp: p., 109:12, 195:10; holp, p.part., 161:3 [O.E. *helpan*]

helte: v., pour , p., 163:10 [O.E. *hyldan*]

hend, hende: a) adv., close, near; him be hende: next to him, close by him, 128:11; me hende: close to me, 129:11; the hende: near you, 143:11
b) adj., gracious, noble, valiant, 1:2, 1:7, 2:4, etc.; used as sb., 31:4, 98:1, 123:6, etc. [O.E. *(ge)hende*]

hendely, hendly, henlyche: adv., graciously, kindly, courteously, 56:2, 155:2, 162:3 [From adj. *hende*]

hendye: adj., courteous, 57:1 [From adj. *hende*]

hens: adv., hence, away, from here, 78:5 [O.E. *heonon*]

hent, hente: v., seize, grasp, p., 163:1, 167:2,8, etc. [O.E. *hentan*]

her, here: a) adv., here, 78:11, 69:5, 78:5, etc. [O.E. *hēr*]
b) See he

herde: See hard

here: sb., hair, 7:9 [O.E. *hǣr*]

here: v., hear, inf: 1:10, 2:12, 14:1, etc.; herd, herde: p. and p.part.,

61:4, 103:3, 105:2, etc.; **herdest:** 2 sing. p., 157:12 [O.E. *hīeran*]

herkeneth, herkenyth, herkneth: v., listen, pay attention, imp., 1:2, 2:12, 98:1, etc. [O.E. *heorcnian*]

heron: adv., in **loke hereon:** take care of this, 26:11 [From *her + on*]

hert, herte: sb., heart, 21:12, 39:5,8, etc. [O.E. *heorte*]

hes: See **he**

hete: See **hight**

heven, hevene: sb., heaven, 179:8, 191:8, 201:11; esp. in expr. **(Jhesu) heven king,** Jesus King of heaven, 3:11, 11:8, 26:9, etc. [O.E. *heofon*]

hew, hewe: v., strike, cut, hew, p., 107:11, 108:7, 111:4 [O.E. *hēawan*]

hewe: sb., colouring, hue, 7:9 [O.E. *hīw*]

hide: a) sb., skin, complexion, 7:9 [O.E. *hȳd*]
b) v., hide, conceal, inf., 23:4, 41:9, 42:10 [O.E. *hȳdan*]

hider: adv., hither, to this place, 101:7 [O.E. *hider*]

hight, hete: v., promise, be called, named, p., 4:1, 35:8, 60:12, etc.; **yhote:** p.part., 128:6* [O.E. *hātan*]

hight, hye, hyghe, hyght: adj., high, exalted, 4:2, 48:3, 51:12, etc. [O.E. *hēah*]

hild: See **hold**

hire, her, here, hes, his, hit: See **he**

hold, holde: v., hold, keep, consider, behold, inf. and pres., 9:1, 54:6, 60:12, etc.; **halde, held,**

hild: p., 13:12, 97:10, 169:6, etc.; **holde, yhold, yholde:** p.part., 35:5, 37:11, 197:3, etc. [O.E. *healdan*]

hold: adj., faithful, loyal, 13:7, 79:9 [O.E. *hold*]

hole: sb., hole, opening, 63:4 [O.E. *hol*]

hole: adj., healthy, well, cured, 179:12, 194:8, 195:1 [O.E. *hāl*]

holp: See **help**

holtys: sb., forest, wood, pl., 42:3 [O.E. *holt*]

home: adv. and sb., home, 22:10, 27:11, 41:12, etc. [O.E. *hām*]

homeward: adv., homeward, 190:2 [From sb. *home*]

hond, honde: sb., hand, 17:4, 18:3, 27:8, etc.; **honden, hondes, honds, hondys,** pl., 67:12, 70:7, 127:10, etc. [O.E. *hand*]

honest: adj., splendid, seemly, 34:4 [O.Fr. *honeste*]

hong, honge: v., hang, be hanged, inf. and p.part., 51:12, 65:6, 68:6, etc. [O.E. *hangian*]

honger: sb., hunger, famine, 135:8, 140:9, 143:12, etc. [O.E. *hungor*]

hongred: v., be hungry, p.part., 153:12 [O.E. *hyngran*]

honour: sb., honour, praise, 1:6, 6:12, 27:11, etc. [O.Fr. *honour*]

honourd: v., honour, p.part.,119:5, 123:6 [O.Fr. *honorer*]

hope: a) sb., hope, 91:7 [O.E. *hopa*]
b) v., trust, expect, hope, pres., 122:10, 186:11, 188:10 [O.E. *hopian*]

hors: sb., horse, sg. and pl., 14:11, 23:3,12, etc. [O.E. *hors*]

hou: See **how**

houndes: sb., hounds, dogs, pl., 42:2 [O.E. *hund*]

hoved: v., mount, p., 99:1 [O.E. *hebban*]

how, howe, hou: adv., how, 1:11, 2:1,4, etc. [O.E. *hū*]

hundred: card. num., hundred, 20:6, 56:11, 115:11, etc. [O.E. *hundred*]

hunt: v., hunt, inf., 42:3 [O.E. *huntian*]

huntyng: sb., hunt, hunting, 12:4, 41:5, 55:4, etc. [O.E. *huntung*]

hurt: sb., pain, 23:4* [? O.Fr. *hurt*/O.E. **hyrtan*]

hyde: v., hide, inf., 66:9 [O.E. *hȳdan*]

hye, hyght: See **hight**

hym, hyt: See **he**

I: pers. pron. 1 sing., nom., 32:7, 52:9, 53:12, etc.; **me**: obl., 1:2, 19:3, 21:10, etc.; **my, myn, myne**: poss. pron., 4:3, 19:6, 21:11, etc.; **myselfe**: refl., 65:10, 69:10 [O.E.]

ibrought: See **breng**

ilk, ilke, ylk, ylke: adj., same, very, 43:9, 65:2, 68:8, etc. [O.E. *ilca*]

ileyde, ilyen: See **lay, layn**

in, inne, yn: prep., in, into, 1:1,9,11, etc. [O.E. *in*]

insame: adv., together, in a group, in company, 89:9, 117:10 [From O.E. *samen*]

into: prep., in, into, to, 15:7, 27:7,8, etc. [O.E. *intō*]

iwisse, iwys, ywis, ywys, ywysse: adv., certainly, indeed, 1:12, 4:7, 5:7, etc. [O.E. *gewisse*]

jentyll, jeste: See **gentil, geste**

joie, joye: sb., joy, happiness, 22:9, 34:10, 43:11, etc. [O.Fr. *joie*]

jorne: See **jurnay**

jugement: sb., judgment, verdict, 98:11, 99:10 [O.Fr. *jugement*]

jurnay, jurne, jorne, jurney: sb., day's work, journey, 21:3, 22:11, 27:6, etc. [O.Fr. *jornee*]

justes: sb., jousts, pl., 15:8 [O.Fr. *jouste*]

justys: sb., judge, judicial court, 106:5 [O.Fr. *justice*]

kare, karfull: See **care, carefull**

karfe: v., cut, carve, p., 185:6 [O.E. *ceorfan*]

kaste: See **caste**

kayes: sb., keys, pl., 182:2,11, 186:4, etc. [O.E. *cǣg*]

kaytyf: sb., wretch, scoundrel, 127:4 [O.Fr. *caitif*]

ken, kend, kende, kynde, kenne, kynne: sb., kin, family, lineage, origin, 1:8, 2:2, 10:2, etc. [O.E. *cynn*/*cynd*]

kend, kende, kynde: adj., kind, gracious, 29:10, 31:2, 123:12, etc. [O.E. *cynde*]

kene: adj., bold, fierce, 127:3, 196:4 [O.E. *cēne*]

kepe: v., keep, guard, care, require, inf., imp. and pres., 26:8, 42:6, 73:11, etc.; **kept**: p.part., 35:11 [O.E. *cēpan*]

kerchyefs: sb., head-cloth, veil, 51:7 [O.Fr. *cuevre chief*]

keste, kiste: See **kysse**

king, kyng: sb., king, 3:11, 11:8, 26:9, etc.; **kinges**: gen. and pl., 49:8, 61:9, 153:1 [O.E. *cyning*] knave: sb., boy, page, attendant, 3:8, 155:8 [O.E. *cnafa*]

knawe, know: v., know, recognise, admit, inf. and p.part., 93:11, 111:1, 165:12, etc.; **knew, knewe, knowe**: p., 8:11, 31:3, 87:5 [O.E. *cnāwan*]

knyfe, knyffe: sb., knife, 127:2, 183:10, 185:2 [late O.E. *cnīf*, from O.N.]

knyght, knight: sb., knight, sing., 2:7, 8:2, 17:3, etc.; **knyghtes**: gen. and pl., 10:10, 14:9, 13:2, etc. [O.E. *cniht*]

kyde: See kyth

kynde, kynne: See kend, ken

kysse: v., kiss, embrace, inf., 119:10; **keste, kiste, kyste**: p., 27:2, 54:9, 62:9, etc. [O.E. *cyssan*]

kyth, kythe, kyde: v., tell, show, make known, inf., 9:9*, 39:6, 45:8, etc. [O.E. *cȳðan*]

lad: See lede

lady: sb., lady, sing., 27:10, 28:2, 76:2, etc.; **ladies, ladyes**: pl., 3:5,7, 6:6, etc.; **ladys**: gen., 129:10 [O.E. *hlǣfdige*]

laid, laide: See lay

lake: sb., pool, 167:9 [O.E. *lacu*]

laked: v., lack, be wanting, p., 20:12 [Prob. O.E. *lak*; cp. M.Du. *lac*]

lapped: v., surround, embrace, p.part., 83:6, 173:4 [From sb. *lappe*]

lappes: sb., hem, lower part of shirt or habergeon, pl., 81:4 [O.E. *læppa*]

lare: sb., teaching, advice, 29:8 [O.E. *lār*]

lasse: See lesse

lasteth: v., last, endure, pres., 201:12 [O.E. *lǣstan*]

lasur, lazar, lazur: sb., leper, 125:8, 129:8, 134:5, etc. [O.Fr. *lazre*]

lawe: sb., law, 51:11, 72:10, 99:12, etc. [O.E. *lagu*]

lay, layn, ley, leyn, lye: v., lay, set, place, hit, inf., 38:5, 49:11, 73:9, etc.; **laid, laide, layd, layn, leid**: p. and p.part., 82:2, 95:15, 120:4, etc.; **layde, leyde, ileyde**: p.part., 39:5, 95:3, 159:9, etc. [O.E. *lecgan*]

layn: v., tell lies, inf., 38:5; **lyeth**: pres., 68:11, 69:6; **ilyen**: p.part., 68:8 [O.E. *lēogan*]

lazar, lazur: See lasur

leches: sb., physicians, doctors, pl., 115:7 [O.E. *lǣce*]

lede: v., lead, guide, conduct, inf., 99:2, 161:6, 175:7; **lad**: p., 113:7,10*, 200:11; **led**: p.part., 199:7 [O.E. *lǣdan*]

lefe, leve, lyefe: adj., dear, beloved, 11:5, 12:1, 14:5, etc.; **lever**: comp., in expr. (X) **had lever**: (X) would rather, 75:8, 187:5 [O.E. *lēof*]

lefte: See leve

leid: See lay

leme: sb., gleam, light, 44:5 [O.E. *lēoma*]

lemes: sb., limbs, 149:6 [O.E. *lim*]

lemman: sb., beloved, 47:10, 191:2 [O.E. *lēof*, dear, + *mann*, being]

lenger: See long

lept: v., leap, p., 86:2 [O.E. *hlēapan*]

les, lesing, lesyng, lesynge: sb., lie, falsehood, 4:6, 7:10, 27:2, etc. [O.E. *lēas, lēasung*]

lesse, lasse: comp. adj. and sb., lesser, of lower rank, 34:8, 95:7, 113:2, etc.; in expr. lesse and mare, all alike, everybody [O.E. *lǣssa*]

leste: See lasteth

lestne, leste: v., listen, hear, pay heed to, inf., 9:3, 39:3, 102:4, etc.; lestne, lestneth: imp., 28:4, 157:10 [O.E. *hlystan*]

lesyng, lesynge: See les

let, lete, lette: v., let, allow, have (something done), inf., imp., subj. and p., 6:4,11, 10:7, etc.; let(te) be: imp., stop, leave aside: 28:1, 29:9, 137:7 [O.E. *lǣtan*]

lete, lette: v., delay, impede, inf., 46:6, 56:12 [O.E. *lettan*]

lettyng: sb., hindrance, delay, 108:10 [O.E. *letting*]

leve: a) See lefe
b) sb., permission, leave (to take/give -), 9:11, 11:11, 21:2, etc. [O.E. *lēaf*]
c) v., leave, inf., 23:3, 160:5; lefte: p., 181:5, 189:1 [O.E. *lǣfan*]
d) v., live, inf., 47:12, 175:6; leved: p., 13:3, 129:5, 140:4, etc. [late O.E. *leofian*]

lever: See lefe

leveray: sb., allowance of food, 134:2, 135:3 [O.Fr. *livree*]

ley, leyde, leying, leyn: See lay, lye

light, lyght (adoun/of): v., dismount, p., 23:12, 87:8, 109:10, etc.; ylight: p.part., 24:1 [O.E. *līhtan*]

logge: sb., lodge, hut, 131:4, 132:1, 139:5, etc. [O.Fr. *loge*]

loke: a) v., look, look over, take care, supervise, inf. and imp., 26:11, 55:2, 151:4; lokest: 2 sing. pres., 87:11; loked: p., 96:1, 100:7, 171:7 [O.E. *lōcian*]
b) v., lock, enclose, p.part, 40:12 [O.N. *loka*]

lond, londe, land: sb., land, country, landed property, 3:2, 5:11, 6:2, etc.; londes, londis: gen., 51:11, 72:10, 99:12 [O.E. *land*]

long: a) adj., long, 107:8, 127:11 [O.E. *lang*]
b) so - , adv., (such) a long time, (so) far, 51:3, 80:7, 129:5, etc. [O.E. *lange*]

longyng, love - : sb., love-sickness, longing, desire, 40:2 [O.E. *langung*]

loo: adj., low, long, 81:4 [O.N. *lāgr*]

lord, lorde: sb., lord, 25:4, 33:8, 52:7, etc.; lordes, lordys: gen. and pl., 55:2, 56:1, 131:1, etc. [O.E. *hlāford*]

lording, lordyng: sb., nobleman, sir (term of polite address), 41:2, 55:5; lordings, lordyngs: pl., 1:8, 7:6, 10:1, etc. [O.E. *hlāfording*]

loreand: adj., sullen, scowling, 33:8* [cp. M.Du. *loeren*, M.H.G. *lūren*]

lore, loren: v., lose, p.part., 110:3, 172:1, lost: p., 127:5 [O.E. *losian*]

loth, lothe: adj. and sb., hateful, hideous, hostile, reluctant, loath, 8:3, 52:10, 137:6, 154:6; lother: comp., 52:11 [O.E. *lāð*]

love: a) sb., love, 1:1, 12:11, 25:2, etc.
b) adj., favourably disposed, 8:3 [O.E. *lufu*]

loved: v., love, cherish, p., 12:7,8, 15:1 [O.E. *lufian*]

lowe: v., laugh, p., 144:7 [O.E. *hliehhan*]

lye: v., lie, lie down, yield, inf., 122:11; **lye, ly:** imp., 93:5, 188:7; **lyeth:** pres., 155:9, 159:1; **lay, leyn:** p., 40:6, 43:3, 59:5, etc.; **layd:** p.part., 95:13; **layng, leying, lying:** ger., 86:11, 110:5, 162:9 [O.E. *licgan*]

lyche, lyke, like: adj., alike, similar, 7:8, 8:4,7, etc. [O.E. *gelīc*/ O.N. *līkr*]

lyefe: See **lefe**

lyeth, lying: See **layn**

lyfe, lyffe, lyve: a) adj., live, 126:12
b) sb., life, existence, 52:11, 53:3, 74:10, etc.; **lyves,** gen., 133:9, 139:9; in expr. **on lyve:** alive, 141:6 [O.E. *līf*]

lyght:a) v., listen. See **lyth**
b) v., dismount. See **light**
c) adj., light, bright, 87:2, 138:1, 182:10 [O.E. *lēoht*]

lyked: v., like, please, p., 52:2, 105:6 [O.E. *līcian*]

lyme: sb., lime, 199:6 [O.E. *līm*]

lytell: adj., little, unimportant, of low rank, 33:10, 57:10, 63:2, etc. [O.E. *lȳtel*]

lyth, lythe, lyght: v., listen, inf., 9:3, 35:9, 39:3, etc. [O.N. *hlȳða*]

lyve, lyves: See **lyfe**

mad: adj., mad, 160:3 [O.E. p.part. *gemǣdde*]

madame: term of address, Madam, Milady, 38:2, 49:4, 61:1, etc. [O.Fr., *ma dame*]

mai: See **may**

maide, maiden, mayd, mayde: sb., girl, maiden, 37:4, 45:1,7, etc.; **maydens:** pl., 37:5, 38:1, 47:2 [O.E. *mægden*]

maidenhede: sb. virginity, , 62:11 [O.E. *mægdenhād*]

make: v., make, construct, arrange, inf., 6:7, 10:10, 68:12, etc.; **made:** p. and p.part., 16:8,10, 23:8, etc. [O.E. *macian*]

maladye: sb., illness, 41:11, 96:8 [O.Fr. *maladie*]

man: sb., man, person, 5:8, 18:7, 37:10, etc.; **men:** pl., 1:6, 7:5, 9:4, etc. [O.E. *mann*]

mankynde: sb., mankind, humanity, 25:3, 85:10, 180:9 [From *man + kind*]

manner: sb., manner, sort, 9:8 [O.Fr. *maniere*]

many: adj., many, 7:5, 9:12, 34:5, etc. [O.E. *manig*]

mare: See **moche**

mariness: sb., happiness, joy, melody, 56:6* [O.E. *myrgnes*]

massanger, messanger: sb., messenger, 18:3, 143:5, 197:7 [O.Fr. *messager*]

may: a) sb., maiden, virgin, 39:11, 40:1, 54:9, etc. [O.E. *mæg*]
b) See **mow**

mayn: sb., power, strength, 109:3, 159:2 [O.E. *mægen*]

mayne: sb., household, 16:11 [O.Fr. *maisnie*]

mede: sb., payment, reward, 3:12, 78:10, 118:2, etc. [O.E. $m\bar{e}d$]

meles: sb., meal, gen., 130:11 [O.E. $m\bar{æ}l$]

melodie: sb., music, melody, 9:7 [O.Fr. *melodie*]

menstralsye: sb., minstrelcy, 9:8 [O.Fr. *menestralsie*]

merthes: See myrth.

mery, merye: adj., merry, joyful, pleasant, 37:4, 40:1, 47:1, etc.; meryest: superl., 153:6, 197:9 [O.E. *myrge*]

mete: a) sb., meal, food, 9:5, 34:4; 55:10, etc. [O.E. *mete*]
b) v., meet, come across, inf., 46:9, 91:10; mette: p., 29:2, 76:2 [O.E. $m\bar{e}tan$]

mette: a) See mete
b) v., dream, p., 83:3 [O.E. $m\bar{æ}tan$]

milde, myld, mylde: adj., gentle, friendly, merciful, humble, 5:6, 134:7, 143:7, etc. [O.E. *mild*]

mo: See moche

moche: adj. and adv., much, large, great, 6:10, 34:7, 35:11, etc.; mare, more, mo, moo: comp., 8:10, 10:11, 13:10, etc.; most, moste: superl., 38:6, 104:9, 126:6, etc. [O.E. *mucel, m* $\bar{a}ra$, $m\bar{æ}st$]

mode: sb., mood, mind, courage, disposition, temper, 5:6, 21:7, 46:1, etc. [O.E. $m\bar{o}d$]

moder: sb., mother, 18:5,10, 40:7, etc. [O.E. $m\bar{o}dor$]

molde: sb., earth, 9:5, 153:6, 163:8, etc. [O.E. *molde*]

mone: sb., lament, 47:5, 131:11, 141:5, etc. [From O.E. v. *mænan*; cp. E.Fris. $m\bar{e}ne$]

monk: sb., monk, 50:5 [O.E. *munuc*, from Latin *monachus*]

month: sb., month, 176:10; monthes: pl., 128:10, 135:1, 176:2 [O.E. $m\bar{o}na\delta$]

moo, more: See moche

morn: a) v., mourn, inf., 74:12; morned: p., 74:4; mornyst: 2 sing. pres., 76:5 [O.E. *murnan*]
b) sb., morning, dawn, 138:1, 177:7 [O.E. *morgen*]

mornyng: a) sb., mourning, lamenting, grief, 21:5, 23:8, 29:9, etc. [O.E. *murnung*]
b) sb., morning, 41:1, 147:3 [From *morn*]

morow: sb., morrow, morning, 108:10 [O.E. *morgen*]

most, moste: a) See moche
b) See v. may

mot, mote: v., must, may, pres. and subj., 58:12, 77:6,7, etc.; most, moste, p., 18:11, 75:1, 81:2, etc. [O.E. *$m\bar{o}tan$]

mouthes: sb., mouth, pl., 11:2 [O.E. muδ]

mow, mowe, may, mai: v., be able to, pres. 2:12, 9:3, 14:1, etc.; might: p., 13:9, 34:10, 39:10, etc. [O.E. *$magan$/*$mugan$]

mydwynter: sb., midwinter, Christmas, 152:3 [O.E. *midwinter*]

myght: a) sb., might, power, strength, 54:2, 71:4, 72:2, etc. [O.E. *miht*]
b) See mow

mykill: adj., great, 33:12 [O.E. *micel*, O.N. *mikil*]

mykyll: sb., size, 20:8 [O.E. *micelu*]

myld, mylde: See milde

myle: sb., mile, 78:5, 131:5, 138:9; **myles:** pl., 141:9 [O.E. *mīl*, from Latin]

myn, myne: See **I**

mynde: sb., mind, thought, 62:1, 176:9 [O.E. *gemynd*]

myrth: mirth, rejoicing, delight, 6:12, 9:5, 43:11, etc.; **merthes:** pl., 45:6; 56:6 [O.E. *myrhð*]

myschaunce: sb., misadventure, 127:8 [O.Fr. *mescheance*]

mysseid: v., slander, reproach, p., 122:2 [From v. *sayn*]

na, nay, no: adv., conj. and interj., no, nor, not, 8:1,2,3, etc. [O.E. *nā*]

naked: adj., naked, bare, 159:4 [O.E. *nacod*]

nam: v., take, betake oneself, go, p., 59:6, 62:8, 81:7; **nome:** p.part., 190:10, 197:7 [O.E. *niman*]

namare, nemo, nomo: adv., never again, no more, no longer, 97:11, 146:9, 149:12, etc. [From adv. *no* + *more*]

name: sb., name, 35:8, 65:5, 105:7, etc.; **names:** pl., 2:11, 4:1 [O.E. *nama*]

nat, not, notte, noght, nought: pron. and adv., nothing, not, 20:12, 25:4, 30:11, etc. [O.E. *nāwiht*]

ne: adv. and conj., not, nor, 7:12, 8:8,10, etc. [O.E. *ne*]

nede: a) sb., need, duty, emergency, distress, 13:7, 14:10, 24:9, etc. [O.E. *nēod, nīed*]
b) **nede, nedys, nethes:** adv., by necessity, inevitably, 75:1, 81:2, 139:1, etc. [O.E. *nīede*]

nemo: See **namare**

nether, nother: pron. and conj., neither, nor, 8:3,8, 12:9, etc. [O.E. *nāhwæðer*]

nethes: See adv. **nede**

never: adv., never, 7:12, 8:10, 12:8, etc. [O.E. *næfre*]

newe: adj., new, another, 31:12, 48:8 [O.E. *nīwe*]

noble: adj., noble, 170:2; **noblest:** superl., 37:10 [O.Fr. *noble*]

noght, nought: a) See **nat**
b) sb., nothing , 20:12, 41:9, 74:10, etc. [O.E. *nāht*]

nome: See **nam**

non, none: pron., none, nobody, 5:2,11, 12:11, etc. [O.E. *nān*]

none: sb., noon, early afternoon (approx. 3 p.m.), 108:10 [O.E. *nōn*, from Latin *nona (hora)*]

norcery: sb., nursery, 182:2 [O.Fr. *norrisserie*]

note: sb., melody, song, 44:8 [O.Fr. *note*]

nother: See **nether**

nothing: adv. and pron., not at all, in no way, nothing, 40:5, 56:12, 57:3, etc. [O.E. *nāðinc*]

notte, not: See **nat**

nought: See **noght**

now, nowe: adv., now, 24:10, 25:9, 28:1, etc. [O.E. *nū*]

nye, nyght: v., approach, come near to, inf., 96:11, 120:6 [O.E.; cp. O.S. *nāhian*. Forms influenced by M.E. adj. *nygh*]

nyghe: a) adv., almost, 48:6 [O.E. *nēah*]
b) See **nyght**

nyght, nyghe: sb., night, 4:4, 13:4, 31:11, etc. [O.E. *niht*]

nyghtyngale: sb., nightingale, 44:8 [O.E. *nihtegala*]

o, on: a) adj., card. num. and pron., one, the same, 4:4,5,7, etc. [O.E. *ān*]
b) **o:** interj., oh, 136:7, 137:1, 169:7, etc.
of, off: a) prep., of, 1:5,6,8, etc.
b) adv., off, away, 23:12, 87:8, 109:10, etc. [O.E. *of*]
ofte: adv., often, frequently, 11:10, 53:8, 75:10, etc. [O.E. *oft*]
old, olde: adj., old, 5:7,10, 7:4, etc. [O.E. *eald*]
on: a) See **o**
b) **on, a, an,** prep. and adv., on, in, at, 4:4,5, 9:5, etc. [O.E. *on*]
onder: See **under**
onys: adv., once, at one time, 31:4 [O.E. *ǣnes*]
orchard: sb., walled garden, orchard, 45:2, 76:3 [O.E. *ortgeard*]
ospryng: sb., ancestry, descent, (offspring), 4:12 [O.E. *ofspring*]
oth: sb., oath, 75:3; **othis:** pl., 161:5 [O.E. *āð*]
other, othir, or: a) conj., or, 15:8, 39:7, 50:4, etc. [O.E. *ōðer*]
b) pron., other, either (one of two), 4:10, 13:11, 24:8, etc. [O.E. *ōðer*, confused in some senses with *āhwæðer*]
out, oute: prep.and adv., out, 19:6, 23:6, 37:2, etc. [O.E. *ūt, ūte*]
outestode: v., fly out (of sparks of fire), p., 108:6 [From v. *stand*]
over: adv., over, above, 16:9, 36:8, 109:1, etc. [O.E. *ofer*]

overcome: v., overcome, defeat, inf. and p.part., 79:12, 80:10 [O.E. *ofercuman*]
overgon: v., pass, go over, inf., 68:2 [O.E. *overgān*]
overtake: v., overtake, inf., 167:6 [From v. *take*]

page: sb., page-boy, servant, 162:11 [O.Fr. *page*]
paleys: sb., palace, 114:1 [O.Fr. *palais*]
palfray: sb., palfrey, saddle-horse, 196:6 [O.Fr. *palefrei*]
parage: sb., descent, rank, 157:5 [O.Fr. *parage*]
paramour: adv., fervently, 1:2 [O.Fr. *par amour*, "for love"]
paraunter: adv., perchance, 161:2 [O.Fr. *par aventure*]
parson: sb., parson, priest, 50:5 [O.Fr. *persone*]
parte: v., separate, part, inf., 23:10; **part:** subj., 48:11 [O.Fr. *partir*]
parting, partyng: sb., parting, separation, 26:12, 27:1, 166:6 [From v. *part*]
passion: sb., Passion (of Christ), 103:5, 170:5 [O.Fr. *passion*, from Latin]
payn: sb., pain, suffering, 40:11; **peynes:** pl., 51:6 [O.Fr. *peine*]
pees, pes: sb., peace, silence, esp. in expr. **hold (one's) p.** , keep quiet, 85:8, 190:8 [O.Fr. *pais*]
pens: sb., penny, coin, pl., 149:8 [O.E. *pening*]
people: sb., people, crowd, 106:7, 169:1 [O.Fr. *peuple*]
pere, piere: sb., peer, equal, 38:8, 154:12 [O.Fr. *per*]

perell: sb., peril, danger, 84:8
[O.Fr. *peril*]

plas: sb., place, spot, 175:2 [O.Fr.
place]

plate: sb., armour plates, 102:8
[O.Fr. *plate*]

play, pley: a) sb., play, game,
sport, 58:2, 152:4, 194:9, etc.
[O.E. *plega*]
b) v., play, amuse oneself, inf.,
76:1, 154:3; pleide, pleyde: p.,
62:10, 183:6 [O.E. *plegan*]

playn: sb., plain, 23:11, 117:9
[O.Fr. *plaigne*]

playng: sb., in expr. in my p. , at
my leasure, enjoying myself, 158:6
[Ger. of *play*]

plight, plyght: a) v., plight,
engage, pledge, promise, inf., imp.
and p., 30:3, 31:4, 48:7, etc.;
plight, plyght, yplyght:
p.part., 2:8, 24:5, 30:7, etc.
b) in plyght, yplyght : adv., in
truth, truly, 39:1, 132:4, 188:4
[O.E. *plihtan*]

poste, postee: sb., power, 125:3,
124:8 [O.Fr. *poesté*]

pouer, poure, power: adj., poor,
8:8, 61:10, 62:4, etc. [O.Fr. *povre*]

pound: sb., pound (monetary unit),
pl., 20:6 [O.E. *pund*]

poverte: sb., poverty, 104:5, 140:4
[O.Fr. *poverté*]

pray: v., pray, ask earnestly, beg,
inf., imp. and pres., 1:2, 65:3,
68:3, etc. [O.Fr. *prier*]

prayere: sb., prayer, 189:12 [O.Fr.
priere]

preche: v., preach, expound in a
tiresome manner, inf., 50:10;
prechest: 2 sing. pres., 50:6
[O.Fr. *prechier*]

preching: sb., preaching, moral-
izing, 51:2 [From ger. of v. *preche*]

prede, pryde: sb., honour, splen-
dour, glory, magnificence, pride,
10:12, 14:12, 34:9, etc. [Late O.E.
prȳte, from adj. *prūd*]

prees: sb., crowd, company, 56:5,
153:8 [O.Fr. presse]

preked, pryked: v., prick (with
spurs), spur on, p., 80:5,7, 98:4,
etc.; prekyng: ger., 100:9 [O.E.
prician]

present, in -: adv., in this place, in
person, at this time, at once, 42:5,
99:8 [From O.Fr. expr. *en present*]

preson: sb., jail, prison, 71:10,
72:6 [O.Fr. *prison*]

preste: sb., priest, 50:4 [O.E
prēost]

preve, prove: v., prove, test,
check, confirm, attempt, try, inf.,
65:11, 68:10, 138:10; preved,
proved: p., 17:4,11, 28:11, etc.
[O.Fr. *prover*]

prevely: adv., secretly, 182:4 [From
O.Fr. adj. *privé*]

price, prys, pryse: sb., prize, high
esteem, 1:9, 6:3, 12:5, etc. [O.Fr.
pris]

prince: sb., prince, 41:3, 97:3,
113:12, etc.; princes: pl., 56:5
[O.Fr. *prince*]

processioun: sb., procession,
113:8 [O.Fr. *procession*]

proud, proude, proued: adj.,
proud, 10:12, 14:12, 34:9, etc.
[O.E. *prūd*]

pryde: See prede

pryked: See preked

pryve: adj., secret, 131:4 [O.Fr.
privé]

pryvyte: sb., private thoughts, secret, 179:6 [O.Fr. *priveté*]

puere: sb., power, strength, 195:2 [O.Fr. *pooir*]

quentelye: adv., skilfully, cleverly, 20:9 [From O.F. *coint*]

quethe: sb., evil, 199:11 [O.E. *cwēad*, dirt]

quite: adj., quit, free, 68:12, 69:3 [O.Fr. *quite*]

quited: v., pay for, requite, p., 3:12 [O.Fr. *quiter*]

rade: See ride

rage: v., be mad, enraged, 157:1 [O.Fr. *rager*]

ran: v., run, p., 59:12, 66:2, 69:7, etc. [O.E. *rinnan*; cp. O.N. *renna*]

rape: sb., haste, 53:8 [O.N. *hrapa*]

raughte, v., grasp, catch, p., 198:7* [O.E. *rǣcan*]

rawe: sb., row, line, 153:4 [O.E. *rǣw*]

rayn: sb., rain, 145:12 [O.E. *regn*]

receyve: v., receive, take possession of, inf., 18:12 [O.Fr. *receveir*]

rechely: adv., quickly, 86:1 [From sb. *reke*, haste]

rede: a) v., read, protect, imp. and pres., 3:3, 4:2, 12:12, etc. [O.E. *rǣdan*]

b) sb., counsel, advice, solution, 24:3, 30:1, 77:12, etc. [O.E. *rǣd*]

c) See ride

redy: adj., ready, 23:1,3, 69:5, etc. [From O.E. *rǣde*]

refrayne: v., soothe, relieve, inf., 40:8 [O.Fr. *refrener*]

regge: sb., back, 148:8, 149:3 [O.E. *hrycg*; cp. O.N. *hryggr*]

renoun, renown: sb., renown, fame, 4:11, 15:12, 50:1 [O.Fr. *renon*]

reson: sb., reason, talk, mind, 71:11, 97:7 [O.Fr. *raison*]

reuly, rewly: adj., sad, wretched, 111:11, 141:5, 147:2, etc. [O.E. *hrēowlīc*]

rewe: v., regret, grieve, repent, inf., 31:9, 53:8, 169:10 [O.E. *hrēowan*]

rewthe, routh: sb., pity, sorrow, misery, 125:10 [O.N. *hryg ð* / O.E. *hrēow*]

riche, ryche: adj., powerful, of high rank, rich, 6:7, 8:8, 9:1, etc.; rycher: comp., 164:11 [O.Fr. *riche* and O.E. *rīce*]

richely, rychely: adv., richly, lavishly, magnificently, sumptuously, 56:4, 76:10, 102:7 [O.E. *rīclīce*]

ride, ryde; v., ride, inf., 12:4, 15:11, 23:1, etc.; ryding: ger., 100:11 [O.E. *rīdan*]

right, ryght: a) sb., justice, right, 13:5, 74:8, 77:4, [O.E. *riht*]

b) adv., right, directly, properly, exactly, (often used as intensifier); 4:2, 8:5, 12:12, etc. [O.E. *rihte*]

robe: sb., clothes, 92:2 [O.Fr. *robe*]

rode: a) p. of ride

b) sb., cross, 32:4, 49:4, 67:4, etc. [O.E. *rōd*]

ron: sb., discourse, counsel, 147:2 [O.E. *rūn*]

roste: sb., roast meat, 101:11 [O.Fr. *rost*]

rote: sb., root, in expr. **hertes r.**, the depths of the heart, 192:7 [O.N. *rōt*]

rought: v., care, reckon, p., 74:10 [O.E. *reccan*]

routh: See rewthe

ry-: See also ri-

ryches: sb., riches, wealth, 62:5 [O.Fr., *richesse*]

ryme: sb., rimed verse, 4:2 [O.Fr. *rime*]

rys: sb., woodland, branch, 12:4 [O.E. *hrīs*]

ryse: v., rise, arise, inf., 177:7 [O.E. *rīsan*]

said, saide, saist: See say

sake: sb., sake, cause, trial, injury, 6:8, 58:10, 100:5, etc. [O.E. *sacu*]

sale: sb., hall [O.E. *sæl*]

sare, sore, soren: adj. and adv., sore, painful, grievous, sorely, cruelly, bitterly, 21:5, 31:9, 57:9, etc. [O.E. *sār*]

sate, sette: See sytte

savage: adj., savage, wild, 157:2 [O.Fr. *sauvage*]

save: a) v., save, redeem, inf. and subj., 25:3, 105:11, 107:6, etc.; **saved**: p., 172:4 [O.Fr. *sauver*] b) prep., save, except, 28:10, 90:5, 115:6, etc. [O.Fr. *sauf*]

savyour: sb., saviour (referring to Christ), 6:9, 38:3 [O.Fr. *salveour*]

saw, sawe: See se

sawe: sb., speech, words, story, 8:6, 99:6 [O.E. *sagu*]

say: See sayn, se

sayn, say, sey, seyn: v., say, inf. and imp. 8:10, 11:2, 38:2, etc.; **saist, seist**: 2 sing. pres., 62:3,

144:6 (future ref.); **said, saide, sayd, seid, seide**: p., 7:10, 18:4,8, etc. [O.E. *secgan*]

schaftes: sb., spear, pl., 107:8 [O.E. *sceaft*]

schall, schull, shall: v., shall, must, 10:10, 22:10, 24:11, etc.; **schallt, schalt**: 2 sing. pres., 19:4, 48:7, 49:6, etc.; **scholde, schuld, schulde**: p., 10:1, 13:6, 23:10, etc. [O.E. **sculan*]

schame: sb., shame, insult, ignominy, 17:11, 64:9, 65:2, etc. [O.E. *scamu*]

schamefully: adv., insultingly, 145:6 [From adj. *shameful*, O.E. *sceomful*]

scharp, sharp: adj., sharp, 66:4, 112:4 [O.E. *scearp*]

sched: v., shed, pour, p., 184:5 [O.E. *scēadan*]

scheld, schelde: sb., shield, 15:11, 99:2, 110:8 [O.E. *scield*]

schend: v., shame, disgrace, injure, inf., 25:12 [O.E. *scendan*]

schette: See schut

schevered: v., break into small pieces, splinter, p., 107:9* [?O.E.; cp. M.Du. *scheveren*]

schild: v., shield, protect, subj., 75:11, 189:7 [O.E. *scieldan*]

schilyng, shilyng: sb., shilling (monetary unit), pl., 147:9, 148:2 [O.E. *scilling*]

scholde: See schall

scholder, schulder: sb., shoulder, 118:8, 112:8, 171:7 [O.E. *sculdor*]

schond, schonde: sb., shame, disgrace, 17:5, 174:6 [O.E. *scand*]

schonye: v., shun, flee from, avoid, inf., 104:11 [O.E. *scunian*]

schope: v., create, p., 85:10 [From p.part. of O.E. *scieppan*] schrede, screde: v., dress, clothe, equip, inf., 76:10, 86:1, 92:2, etc. [O.E. *scrȳdan*]

schrew: sb., wretch, rogue, villain, 92:11 [O.E. *scrēawa*]

schrewd, schrewed: adj., evil, depraved, 127:1, 149:5 [From sb. *schrew*]

schuld: See schall

schut, schette: v., shut, close, bolt (a door), p., 66:8, 186:2 [O.E. *scyttan*]

screde: See schrede

se, see, sen, sene: v., see, inf., 33:5, 35:6, 71:3, etc.; saw, sawe, say, sey: p., 7:12, 39:7, 45:4, etc.; seyn, ysene, sen: p.part., 63:7, 70:12, 127:6 [O.E. *sēon*]

see: a) See se

b) sb., sea, 1:2 [O.E. *sǣ*]

seid, seide, seist: See sayn

seint, seint: adj., saint, holy, 38:3, 62:2, 64:5, etc. [O.Fr. *saint*]

seised, seysed: v., seize, hold, enfeoff, take/give possession of, p., 27:8, 123:8, 200:4 [O.Fr. *saisir*]

seke: adj., sick, ill, 40:6, 43:3, 97:9 [O.E. *sēoc*]

sekerlie: adv., assuredly, truthfully, 96:7 [From O.E. adj. *sicor*]

sekyng: sb., sighing, 21:5 [From ger. of v., O.E. *sīcan*]

self, selfe, selve: adj., self, same, (intensifies pron. or sb.), 47:4, 92:3, 98:7, etc. [O.E. *self*]

selle: v., sell, inf., 146:8; sold, solde: p. and p.part., 91:5, 107:5, 135:7, etc. [O.E. *sellan*]

semely: adj., seemly, fitting, appropriate, handsome, noble, 10:9, 14:6, 34:3, etc.; semelyest: superl., 37:8 [O.N. *soemiligr*]

semyng: adj., seemly, noble, 1:8* [From O.E. v. *sēman*]

sen: See seth, se

send, sende: v., send, inf., 6:4,11, 31:1, etc.; sent: p. and p.part., 93:7, 94:7, 103:6, etc. [O.E. *sendan*]

sene: See se

serjaunt: sb., servant, man-at-arms, attendant, 154:2; serjauntes: pl., 152:10 [O.Fr. *serjant*]

servaunt: sb., retainer, attendant, servant, 36:5, 154:7 [O.Fr. *servant*]

serve: v., serve, inf., 36:6, 132:3,11, etc.; served: p. and p.part., 7:4, 34:7, 56:4, etc. [O.Fr. *servir*]

service, servyse: sb., service, employment, 10:8, 11:6, 160:8 [O.Fr. *service*]

sete: sb., seat, 56:9 [O.E. *set*]

seth, sen, sith, sygh: adv. and conj., since, afterwards, 31:1, 58:10, 70:12, etc. [O.E. *si ð ð an*]

sette, set: a) See sytte

b) v., set, place, p. and p.part., 56:2, 71:2, 98:8, etc. [O.E. *settan*]

sevenyght: sb., seven days, a week, 53:10, 60:5 [cp. O.E. adj. *seofonnihte*]

sey, seyn: See sayn, se

seynt, seysed: See seint, seised

sh-: See sch-

shamely: adv., shamefully, 174:6 [O.E. *scamlic*]

sing: v., sing the divine office, celebrate mass, inf., 201:5 [O.E. *singan*]

sith: See seth

skape: v., escape, inf., 179:11, 198:11 [From var. of O.Fr. *eschaper*] slake: v., relieve, alleviate, inf., 45:3, 67:2 [O.E. *slacian*]

slang: v., sling, throw, p., 167:9 [? O.N.; cp. O.E. *slingan*]

sle, slo, slon: v., slay, kill, inf., 67:11, 84:6, 110:5, etc.; sleyst: 2 sing. p., 169:9; slew, slow: p., 121:7, 122:5, 191:11; slawe, slayn, slayne, slon, slone, yslayn: p.part., 67:7, 83:9*, 89:11, etc. [O.E. *slēan*]

sleppe: sb., sleep, slumber, 81:10 [O.E. *slǣp*]

sloo: sb., sloe, berry, 32:11 [O.E. *slāh*]

slowe: sb., mud, 168:8 [O.E. *slōh*]

smale: adj., small, of low rank, 198:9 [O.E. *smæl*]

smere: v., smear, anoint, inf., 177:10 [O.E. *smierwan*]

smete, smote: v., strike, hit, p. and p.part., 66:5,10, 109:3, etc. [O.E. *smītan*]

so, soo: adv.and conj., so, as, in such a manner, 5:6,12, 8:4, etc. Often used in parenthetic clauses to introduce asseverations, oaths, etc.: so God me spede [O.E. *swā*]

solace: v., comfort, console, 42:9, 43:6 [O.Fr. *solacier*]

sold, solde: See sell

solempnite: sb., solemnity, honour, 27:12, 35:12 [O.Fr. *solemnité*]

som, some: See sume

someres, somers: sb., summer, gen., 34:3, 42:11, 43:9 [O.E. *sumor*]

sonde: sb., message, messenger, (God's) grace, providence, 6:4, 18:6, 131:12, etc. [O.E. *sand*]

sone: a) adv., soon, immediately, 87:5, 99:4, 115:7, etc. [O.E. *sōna*] b) sb., son, 4:7, 49:8, 132:8, etc.; sonnes: pl., 7:2, 10:7, 11:5, etc. [O.E. *sunu*]

song, songe: sb., song, 42:11, 43:10, 80:12, etc. [O.E. *sang*]

soo: See so

sore, soren: See sare

sorow, sorowe: sb., sorrow, grief, 27:1, 40:2, 84:6, etc. [O.E. *sorg*]

sory: adj., sad, sorry, miserable, 87:11, 197:5,11 [O.E. *sārig*]

soth, sothe: a) See seth b) sb., truth, 38:3, 76:6, 168:11, etc.[O.E. *sōð*]

sought: v., seek, look for, p., 190:4 [O.E. *sēcan*]

soule: sb., soul, 77:11 [O.E. *sāwol*]

spake: See speke

spare: v., spare, refrain (from doing something), inf., 57:3, 80:4, 98:3, etc. [O.E. *sparian*]

speche: sb., speech, words, 52:5 [O.E. *spǣc*, var. of *sprǣc*]

spede: v., prosper, promote, give assistance, make succeed, (esp. in expr. so/as God me spede), inf. and subj., 19:3, 24:12, 37:6, etc.; spedde: p., 116:6 [O.E. *spēdan*]

speke: v., speak, inf. and subj., 30:10, 39:11, 40:5, etc.; spekest: imp., 54:3; spake: p., 15:5, 39:9, 73:1, etc. [O.E. *specan*, var. of *sprecan*]

spelle: sb., discourse, words, 53:6 [O.E. *spell*]

spent: v., spend (money), p.part., 149:7 [O.E. *spendan*]

spere: sb., spear, 15:11, 99:2, 100:8, etc. [O.E. *spere*]

sperned: spurn, kick, p., 168:4
[O.E. *spurnan*]
spill, spille, spyll, spylle: v.,
spill, lose, die, inf., 52:5, 53:3,
105:9, etc. [O.E. *spillan*]
spise: sb., contempt, 122:3 [From
O.Fr. *despiser*]
spite, spite: sb., scorn, shame,
105:9, 129:10, 130:4 [Shortened
form of O.Fr. *despit*]
spouse: v., marry, 61:2, 118:2;
spoused: p., 27:10, 123:11,
196:11 [O.Fr. *espouser*]
spraid: v., sprout, spray, p., 108:9
[? From sb. *spray*]
spring: v., spring, jump, spread,
inf. and subj., 27:5, 129:7 [O.E.
springan]
spyll, spylle, spyte: See spill,
spite
squier, squire, squyer: sb., squire,
8:2, 162:2, 163:1, etc.; squiers:
pl., 198:3 [O.Fr. *escuier*]
stant: v., See stonde
state: sb., estate, state, 153:10
[O.Fr. *estat*]
sted, stede: sb., place, 15:4,7,
104:11, etc. [O.E. *stede*]
stede: sb., horse, steed, 15:11, 80:5,
86:2, etc.; stedes: pl.,15:3, 27:5,
107:7 [O.E. *stēda*]
stefe: See styffe
stent, stente: stint, stop, cease, p.,
46:2, 58:9, 101:1, etc. [O.E.
styntan]
sterne: adj., severe, cruel, 108:5
[O.E. *styrne*]
sterte: v., hurry, leap, p., 66:7,
85:1, 167:1, etc. [O.N. *sterta*]
steward: sb., steward, 16:10, 17:2,
25:11, etc. [O.E. *stigweard*]
stodde, stode: See stonde

stole: v., steal, p.part., 166:10
[O.E. *stelan*]
ston, stone: sb., stone, 101:1,
117:5, 186:2, etc. [O.E. *stān*]
stonde: a) See stound
b) v., stand, inf. and subj., 13:9,
51:3, 131:6; stant: pres., 159:4;
stodde, stode: p., 21:8, 26:1,
32:1, etc. [O.E. *standan*]
stound, stounde, stonde: sb.,
moment, 109:8, 111:7, 169:10,
etc. [O.E. *stund*]
stoute: adj., stout, bold, brave,
98:5, 148:4, 195:4, etc. [cp. O.Fr.
estout, M.Du. *stout*]
streight: adv., tight, firmly, 169:6
[O.Fr. *estreit*]
strokes: sb., blows, strokes, pl.,
198:8 [From O.E. v. *strīcan*]
strong: adj., strong, powerful,
resolute, 32:8, 40:11, 51:6, etc.
[O.E. *strang*]
stryfe, stryve: sb., strife, quarrel,
58:9, 134:3, 190:9, etc. [O.Fr.
estrif]
styffe, stefe: adj., stout, brave,
107:7, 169:4 [O.E. *stīf*]
styll, stylle: adj., still, quiet, 49:1,
52:1, 82:4, etc. [O.E. *stille*]
suche: adj. and sb., such, 68:5,
96:8, 186:9 [O.E. *swilc*]
suffred: v., suffer, p., 103:5, 134:9,
170:5 [O.Fr. *sufrir*]
sume, summe, som, some: adj.
and pron., some, certain, 57:11,
84:7, 150:11, etc.; sumdele
mare: somewhat more, 148:10
[O.E. *sum*]
suore: See swore
suster: sb., sister, gen., 132:8 [O.E.
sweostor]
swan: sb., swan, 112:3 [O.E. *swan*]

swayn: sb., swain, young man, 38:4, 67:3, 117:3, etc. [O.E. *swān*]

swerde, sword, sworde: sb., sword, 95:14, 97:6, 112:7, etc.; swerdes: pl., 107:10 [O.E. *sweord*]

swere, swore: v., swear, inf., 75:3, 77:7, 78:8, etc.; suore, swor, swore: p., 32:4, 54:2, 67:4, etc.; sworn: p.part., 107:1, 136:10, 161:5 [O.E. *swerian*]

swete: a) adj., sweet, 56:3, 60:3 b) as sb., sweet maiden, 46:3 c) adv., sweetly, tenderly, 62:9 [O.E. *swēte*]

swevene: sb., sleep, 179:7, 191:7 [O.E. *swefn*]

swonned. v., swoon, faint, p., 21:6; swonyng: ger., 171:10 [O.E. *swōgan*]

sword, sworde: See swerde

swyth, swythe: adv., quickly, 55:7, 59:12, 144:8, etc.; als swythe: immediately, 172:10 [O.E. *swīðe*]

syde: sb.,side, 10:9, 34:6, 82:6, etc. [O.E. *sīde*]

sygh: See seth

syght: sb., sight, vision, aspect, 7:8, 8:4, 37:8, etc. [O.E. *siht*]

syking: sb., sighing, 98:12, 136:3 [From ger. of O.E. v. *sīcan*]

synne: sb., crime, sin, 180:3 [O.E. *synn*]

syre, sire: sb., lord, sir (term of address), 4:8,10, 15:9, etc. [O.Fr. *sire*]

sythe: sb., time, occasion, sing. and pl., 9:12, 39:12, 56:11, etc. [O.E. *sīð*]

sytte: v., sit, inf., 128:11, 129:11; sate, sette: p., 56:9, 58:7, 179:1 [O.E. *sittan*]

take: v., take, touch, seize, inf. and imp., 60:11, 72:4, 91:8, etc.; taken, take: p.part., 18:4, 69:9, 90:2, etc.; toke: p., 9:11, 11:11, 16:5, etc. [O.N. *taka*]

tale: sb., tale, story, speech, 36:9, 188:9 [O.E. *talu*]

talk: v., talk, speak to, 45:12 [M.E., from *tale* or *tell*]

talkyng: sb., talking, narrative, 4:3, 40:4 [From ger. of v. *talk*]

taste: v., examine, inf., 115:8 [O.Fr. *taster*]

taught, taugt: v., teach, instruct, p., 50:10, 118:8 [O.E. *tæcan*]

tel, tell, tyll, tylle: prep., until, 9:10, 23:10, 48:11, etc. [O.N. *til*]

tell, telle: v., tell, narrate, account, inf., imp. and pres., 4:3, 36:9, 65:3, etc.; told, tolde: p., 7:1, 9:4, 16:1, etc.; tolde, ytolde: p.part., 91:1, 124:12, 125:7 [O.E. *tellan*]

tene: sb., injury, vexation, contumely, 127:12 [O.E. *tēona*]

than: a) conj., than, 7:11, 29:12, 34:11, etc. [O.E. *ðonne*] b) See then

thanked: v., thank, give thanks to, p., 9:12, 11:10, 55:12, etc. [O.E. *ðancian*]

thar, thare, ther, there: adv., there, 5:2,11, 7:6, etc.; therate: 152:8, 162:8: there, at that place; therefor, therefore, therfor: therefore, for that reason, 3:11, 60:7, 77:5, etc.; therin: therein, in there, 131:10, 149:11, 199:7;

therof: thereof, because of this, 17:9, 32:11, 57:9, etc.; theron: 138:12*; therto: thereto, 137:12, in favour of, 13:12, (ready) for it, 69:5, therwith, therewith: therewith, with this 147:9,11, 188:2 [O.E. ðær]

that: a) also thet: dem. and rel. pron., that, those, 1:2, 3:6,9, etc.; who that: whoever, 8:9; tho: pl., 126:5
b) dem. adj., that, 3:2, 5:9, 5:11, etc.
c) part of compound conj.: ffor that, because, 45:9; sith that, since, 31:3; tyll that, until, 23:10, whather that: whether, 26:5; wher that, wherever, 39:7 [O.E. ðæt]

thaugh, thaught, thoght, though, thowgh: adv. and conj., though, even though, even if, if, 50:12, 70:3, 91:9, etc.; thaugh who: whoever, 127:9 [O.E. ðēah]

the: a) def. art.: See tho
b) pers. pron.: See thou
c) v., prosper, succeed, in expr., so mote I the, 157:11 [O.E. ðēon]

theder: adv., thither, over there, 6:11, 150:9 [O.E. ðider]

thee: See tho

thefe: sb., thief, criminal, 64:7 [O.E. ðēof]

ther, there: See he, thar

then, thenne, than, tho, thoo: conj. and adv., then, when, 3:8, 5:1, 12:7, etc. [O.E. ðon]

thenk: v., think, think of, remember, imp., 25:8, 26:11, 49:7, etc.; thought: p., 45:10, 46:4, 52:4, etc.; me think, him/here thought: impers. constr., it seems

to me, it seemed to him/her, 39:8, 42:12, 47:11, etc.; thei thoughten hem: 41:4* [O.E. ðencan]

thens, thense: adv., thence, from there, 82:10, 141:9 [M.E.]

ther-, ther, there: See thar -, that, he

thes, these: See this

thet: See that

thi, thin: See thou

thing: sb., thing, 25:1,10, 46:6, etc.; in all t. : in every respect, 3:10, 8:7, 20:10, etc. [O.E. ðing]

this: dem. art. and pron., this, 22:12, 24:7, 26:10, etc.; thes, these, this: pl., 3:7, 73:7, 101:5, etc. [O.E. ðeos]

tho, thoo: a) def. art., also the, thee, 1:2,10, 2:3, etc. [O.E.]
b) dem. pron.: See that
c) conj. and adv.: See then

thoght: See thaugh

thorght, thoroght, thorought: See thorow

thorn: sb., thorn, 25:2 [O.E. ðorn]

thorow, thorowght, thorght, thoroght, thorought: prep., through, thanks to, because of, 18:6, 66:11, 108:8, etc. [O.E. ðurh]

thou, thow, thowe: pers. pron. 2 sing., nom., 19:4, 25:5, 26:8, etc.; the: obl., thee; 21:10, 24:11, 25:1, etc.; thi, thin, thyn: poss., 22:10, 25:4, 29:5, etc. [O.E.]

though, thowgh: See thaugh

thought: a) sb., thought, worry, desire, 20:3, 21:4, 51:4, etc. [O.E. ðoht]
b) also thoughten: See thenk

thow, thowe: See thou

thre, three: card. number, three, 21:12, 47:11, 79:12, etc. [O.E. *ðre*]

throtes: sb., throat, pl.,185:6 [O.E. *ðrote*]

thryfe, thryve, tryve: v., thrive, prosper, inf., 5:1, 58:12, 134:6, [O.N. *ðrīfa*]

thurst: v., be able to, p., 97:11 [O.E. *ðurfan*]

thus: adv., thus, in this way, 12:1, 14:1, 33:1, etc. [O.E. *ðus*]

to, too: prep., adv. and conj., to, for, at, 1:2,10, 3:5, etc. [O.E. *tō*]

today: adv. and sb., today, on this very day, 101:7, 114:8 [From *day*]

todrawe: v., draw apart, tear, p.part., 51:10, 72:11 [From *drawe*]

to-fonde: v., find, p.part. in expr. free to-fonde, most noble, 3:5*, 110:7, 193:6 [From *find*]

tofore: prep., in front of, before, 143:2 [O.E. *tōforan*]

tohide: v., hide completely, p.part, 63:3 [From *hide*]

togeder, togider, togyder: adv., together, mutually, 13:2,7, 27:2, etc. [O.E. *tōgædre*]

toke: See take

tokne: sb., token, sign, 26:12, 166:6 [O.E. *tācen*]

told, tolde: See tell

tomorn: adv. and sb., tomorrow, 79:2, 192:11 [O.E. *tōmorgen*]

tonge: sb., tongue, 152:2 [O.E. *tunge*]

tonyght: adv. and sb., at night, last night, 179:7, 191:7 [From *night*]

tonne: sb., cask, 100:5 [O.E. *tunne*]

too: See to

torente: v., tear in pieces, inf., 51:8 [O.E. *tōrendan*]

tornement: sb., tournament, 15:8 [O.Fr. *tornoiement*]

toun, town: sb., town, 1:9, 6:3, 15:6, etc.; townes: gen., 139:4 [O.E. *tūn*]

toure, towre: sb., tower, castle, 1:9, 6:3, 15:5, etc. [O.Fr. *tour*]

trad: v., tread, trample, p., 167:10, 168:8 [O.E. *tredan*]

traitour, tratour, traytour, treitour, tretour, treytour: sb., traitor, 32:5, 64:10, 65:8, etc. [O.Fr. *traitre, traitor*]

tre, tree: sb., tree, 68:6,11, 82:2 [O.E. *trēow*]

trechery, trecherye: sb., treachery, 17:6, 88:8 [O.Fr. *tricherie*]

treitour, tretour: See traitour

treson: sb., treason, 25:7, 33:11, 57:11, etc. [O.Fr. *traïson*]

trew, trewe: adj., true, loyal, faithful, 3:10, 10:4, 24:10, etc.; trewer: comp., 12:11 [O.E. *trēowe*]

trewly: adv., truly, faithfully, 36:9, 60:11, 156:3 [O.E. *trēowlic*]

trewth, trewthe, trouth, trowth: sb., troth, faith, loyalty, 2:8, 13:2, 24:5, etc.; trewthes, trouthes, trowthes: pl., 30:3, 54:8, 60:6 [O.E. *trēowð*]

trey: sb., affliction, grief, 127:12 [O.E. *trega*]

treytour: See traitour

trinyte: sb., Holy Trinity, 1:1 [O.Fr. *trinité*]

trompettes: sb., trumpet, pl., 153:2 [O.Fr. *trompette*]

trouth, trouthes, trowth, trowthes: See trewth

trust: v., trust, confide, have confidence in, inf., 29:8 [O.N. *treysta*]

tryve: See thryfe

turne: v., turn, change, inf., 53:9; turned: p. and p.part., 96:6, 184:2 [O.E. *tyrnan*]

tway, twayn, twey, two, twoo: card. num., two, 1:5,10, 3:4, etc. [O.E. *twēgen*]

twelf: card. num., twelve, 133:2* [O.E. *twelf*]

twenty: card. num., twenty, 71:9 [O.E. *twēntig*]

tyde: sb., time, season, hour, 10:3, 14:9, 23:2, etc.; often in expr. as tyde, immediately [O.E. *tīd*]

tyght: v., determine, arrange, p. part., 138:5 [? cp. Germ. *tichten*]

tyll, tylle: See tel

tymber: sb., timber, wood, 131:2 [O.E. *timber*]

tyme: sb., time, 6:1, 34:1, 87:3, etc. [O.E. *tīma*]

tyre: sb., attire, clothing, equipment, 102:9 [from O.Fr. v. *atirier*]

tything: sb., message, tidings, news, 137:8 [O.N. *tī ðindi*]

unhende: adj., discourteous, rude, 169:8 [From adj. *hende*]

unknow: adj., unrelated, 2:2 [From adj. *know*]

unkynde: adj., unkind, unnatural, 101:12, 169:7; unkender: comp., 172:2 [From adj. *kend*]

unryght: sb., injustice, 49:10, 101:10, 122:4 [O.E. *unriht*]

unto: prep., unto, to, 109:5 [M.E]

up: prep. and adv., up, 13:12, 72:8, 81:4, etc. [O.E. *up*]

upholde, holde up: v., uphold, support, maintain, inf., 73:5, 72:8; halde up: pret., 13:12 [From O.E. *healdan*]

upon, uppon: prep. upon, over, 3:7, 23:11, 49:11, etc. [O.E. *uppan*]

upryght: adj., upright, in vertical position, 169:6 [O.E. *upriht*]

us: See we

verament, verrament: adv., truly, in truth, 42:4, 143:4, 149:8, etc. [O.Fr. *veraiment*]

visage: sb., face, visage, 157:4 [O.Fr. *visage*]

voys: sb., voice, 103:2 [O.Fr. *vois*]

under, onder: prep. and adv., under, beneath, 12:4, 42:10, 45:2, etc. [O.E. *under*]

underfong: v., undertake, accept, inf. and subj., 79:10, 98:11, 103:7 [O.E. *underfōn*]

understond, understonde: v., understand, perceive, inf. and pres., 3:1, 6:1, 17:1, etc. [O.E. *understandan*]

wade: v., advance, move, go, inf., 112:7 [O.E. *wadan*]

wai, way, wey: sb., way, direction, 11:11, 23:7, 59:2, etc. [O.E. *weg*]

wake: v., be awake, keep watch, 156:9 [O.E. *wacian*, O.N. *vaka*]

walke: v., walk, inf., 156:9; walked: p., 45:2 [O.E *wealcan*]

wan: a) adj., pale, wan, 197:10 [O.E. *wann*]

b) also wanne: See wynne

warant: sb., warrant, surety, 79:4
[O.Fr. *garant*]

ware: a) adj., wary, prudent, 13:1,
16:2 [O.E. *wær*]
b) also waren: See ben

warn, warne: v., warn, inf. and
pres. ind., 25:1, 32:7, 64:6, etc.;
warned: p., 178:3 [O.E. *warnian*]

water: sb., water, 199:8 [O.E.
wæter]

wax, wex: v., grow, become, inf.,
197:5, 140:8; wax, waxe, wex,
wexe, woxe: p., 32:2, 65:1, 66:1,
etc.; wexith: pres., 137:6; wox:
p.part., 195:2 [O.E. *weaxan*]

wayn: See wynne, wayne

wayne, wayn: sb., cart, 159:1,
160:5, 162:9, etc. [O.E. *wægn*]

wayted: v., await, p., 117:8 [O.Fr.
gaitier]

wed: v., wed, marry, inf., 61:10
[O.E. *weddian*]

wede: sb., clothing, 3:6, 12:6,
14:11, etc. [O.E. *wǣd*]

we, wee: pers. pron. 1 pl., nom.,
3:3, 12:12, 24:5, etc.; us: obl.,
48:11, 60:10, 68:8, etc.; oure:
poss. pron. and adj., 6:9, 26:12,
30:3, etc. [O.E.]

wel, wele, well: adv., well, very,
10:11, 12:7, 15:1, etc. [O.E. *wel*]

welaway, welawey: interj., alas!,
80:12, 147:4, 171:6, etc. [From
O.E. *weg-lā*]

wele, well: a) sb., prosperity,
happiness, 1:11, 2:1, 13:5, etc.
[O.E. *wela*]
b) See wel

wem: sb., injury, blemish, 194:7
[O.E. *wamm*]

wen, won: sb., opulence,
expectation, 67:10, 81:11, 180:12
[O.E. *wēn*]

wend, wende: a) See wene
b) also won, wonde: v., go,
travel, depart, flee, fear, hesitate,
inf., imp. and p., 2:1, 10:1, 18:11,
etc. [O.E. *wendan*]

wending: sb., departure, 29:7 [O.E.
wendung]

wene: v., think, believe, inf. and p.,
93:10, 95:3,6, 96:3, etc. [O.E.
wēnan]

wenst, went, wente: See gan

weped, wept, wepte: v., weep,
mourn over, p. and p.part., 39:12,
70:7, 130:7, etc.; wepyng: ger.,
172:12 [O.E. *wēpan*]

wepen: sb., armour, weapon, 14:11
[O.E. *wǣpen*]

weping: sb., weeping [From ger. of
v., O.E. *wēpan*]

were, weren: See ben

werke: v., work, make, inf., 20:5;
wroght, wrought, wrouth: p.
and p.part., 20:9, 33:11, 87:12, etc.
[O.E. *wyrcan*]

wery: adj., tired, weary, 86:10 [O.E.
wērig]

wes: See ben

wex, wexe, wexith: See wax

wexing: sb., size, growth, 8:5
[From ger. of v., O.E. *weaxan*]

wey: See wai

whan, when, whenne: conj.,
when, 5:4,7,10, etc. [O.E. *hwanne*]

what, whate: rel. pron., what, 1:2,
2:10,11, etc. [O.E. *hwæt*]

whather: pron., which (of two),
26:5 [O.E. *hwæðer*]

wher, where: adv. and conj., where, everywhere, 2:6, 31:5, 39:7, etc. [O.E. _hwǣr_]

wherever: conj. (with subj.), wherever, 161:1 [From _where_ + _ever_]

wheter, whether: adv. and conj., whether (or not), 161:7; w-.... other: whether ... or, 50:4, 58:7, 60:10, etc. [O.E. _hwæ ðer_]

whi, whye: adv.and conj., why, 50:2, 62:3, 76:5, etc. [O.E. _hwȳ_]

whiche: adj., which, in expr. (at) whiche tyme as, at the time when, 177:8, 180:8 [O.E. _hwilc_]

whider: adv., where, in what direction, whither, 126:2, 151:5 [O.E. _hwider_]

while: a) sb., while, time, moment, 33:10, 57:10, 78:1
b) also whiles, whyle: adv. and conj., while, whilst, 13:3,9, 30:10, etc. [O.E. _hwīl_]

whilom: adv., formerly, at one time, 1:2, 3:2, 128:2, etc. [O.E. _hwīlum_]

white: adj., white, 15:3, 112:3 [O.E. _hwīt_]

who: pron., who, whoever, 8:9, 37:7,8, etc.; whome: obl., 155:6 [O.E. _hwȳ_]

whye: See whi

whyle: See while

wife, wiffe, wyffe, wyve: sb., wife, 61:3, 84:3, 104:10, etc. [O.E. _wīf_]

wight, wyght: adj., brave, valiant, 13:1, 36:5, 128:2, etc. [orig. obsc., cp. M.L.G. _wicht_, heavy]

wikked, wyked, wykked: adj., wicked, evil, 32:5, 127:1, 149:5 [From O.E. v. _wīcan_]

will, wille, wyll: v., want, desire, wish (with inf., expr. future), pres., 4:2, 21:12, 25:12, etc.; wilt, wilte, wylt, wylte: 2 pres., 29:8,10, 32:6, etc.; wold, wolde: p., 6:7, 9:11, 15:2, etc. [O.E. _willan_]

wise, wys, wyse: a) adj., wise, 16:2, 24:3,12, etc.;
b) wys: adv., truly, 106:8 [O.E. _wīs_]

wissely: adv., certainly, truly, 75:4 [O.E. _wislīce_]

wiste: See wyt

with, wyth: prep., with, against, 6:12, 9:5, 10:6, etc. [O.E. _wið_]

within, withine, withinne: prep. and adv., within, 18:1, 33:10, 57:10, etc. [O.E. _wi ðinnan_]

without, withoute: a) prep., without, 4:6, 7:10, 22:3, etc.
b) also withouten: adv., outside, 153:11 [O.E. _wi ðūtan_]

wo, woo: a) sb., woe, sadness, adversity, 1:11, 2:1, 13:5, etc.
b) adj., sad, sorrowful, 10:3, 19:5, 20:1, etc. [O.E. _wā_]

wode: adj., mad, 32:2, 63:11, 66:2, etc. [O.E. _wōd_]

wold, wolde: See will

wolves: sb., wolf, pl., 83:8* [O.E. _wulf_]

won: See wen, wend, wone

wonde: See wend

wonder: sb., wonder, marvel, 70:3, 136:8, 174:2, etc. [O.E. _wundor_]

wondes: See wound

wone, won: sb., dwelling-place, 34:11, 37:2, 41:8, etc. [O.E. _wuna_] woneth: v., dwell, pres., 78:5, 142:6.; woned: p., 6:2, 82:10, 141:8 [O.E. *wunian*]

wont: adj., accustomed, 96:5 [From O.E. v. *wunian*]

woo: See wo

word, worde: sb., word, speech, message, rumour, 12:9, 13:8, 24:6, etc.; wordes, pl., 17:10, 19:2, 22:2, etc. [O.E. *word*]

wordely: adj. and adv., worthy, splendid, stately, honourable, in a dignified way, 14:11, 37:2, 41:8, etc. [O.E. *weorðlic*]

workes: sb., deed, action, pl., 169:8 [O.E. *weorc*]

world, worlde: sb., world, 46:4, 48:9, 51:1, etc.; worldes, worldys: gen., 67:5,10, 81:11, etc. [O.E. *woruld*]

worldely, worldle: adj., worldly/ worthy (ambiguous), 34:11, 180:12, 159:12; See also wordely, worldly

worldly: adj., worldly, earthly, of this world, 160:9 [O.E. *woruldlic*]

worse, worst: See evell

worthi: adj., honourable, worthy (of), 3:6, 94:8, 102:8, etc.; worthiest: superl., 12:6, 37:9, 38:11 [From O.E. *weorð*]

wote: v., know, pres., 172:3 [O.E. *witan*]

wound, wounde: sb., wound, injury, 111:8,10, 115:8, etc.; wondes, woundes: pl., 108:8, 114:9, 134:9 [O.E. *wund*]

wox, woxe: See wax

wrake: sb., distress, enmity, 58:11, 69:6, 84:5, etc. [O.E *wracu*]

wrath, wreth, wroth: a) sb., anger, wrath, 32:2, 33:1,2, etc.

b) adv., angry, 129:4 [O.E. *ræððo*]

wrayen: v., reveal, betray, inf., 64:3; wray: imp. and subj., 120:12, 151:4 [O.E. *wrēgan*]

wrecche, wreche: sb., wretch, 104:4, 199:11 [O.E. *wræcca*]

wreched, wrecched: adj., wretched, miserable, 127:4, 137:4 [M.E., from *wrecche*]

wreth: See wrath

wroght: See werke

wrong: a) adj. and sb., wrong, injustice, 13:5, 40:10, 51:9, etc. [O.E. *wrang*]

b) v., wring, twist, p., 70:7, 127:10, 136:2; wryngyng: ger., 174:12 [O.E. *wringan*]

wroth: See wrath

wrought, wrouth: See werke

wy- : See also wi-

wyde: adj., wide, vast, broad, 82:9, 86:9, 108:8 [O.E. *wīd*]

wyght: a) sb., creature, being, 8:1, 60:3, 71:5, etc.; weight, 20:7 [O.E. *wiht*]

b) See adj. wight

wyld, wylde: adj., wild, 52:8, 81:8, 83:8* [O.E. *wilde*]

wyll, wylle: a) sb., will, pleasure, desire, 52:4, 53:12, 54:7, etc. [O.E. *willa*]

b) See v. will

wyn, wyne: a) sb., wine, 162:5,11, 163:3, etc. [O.E. *wīn*]

b) sb., trouble, strife, 33:8* [O.E. *winn*]

wynd: sb., wind, 145:12 [O.E. *wind*]

wynne: v., win, gain, inf, 81:11, 156:11; wan, wanne, wayn: p.,

149

62:11, 121:2, 151:2, etc. [O.E. *winnan*]

wynter: sb. winter, year, pl., 133:2*, 148:5 [O.E. *winter*]

wysched: v., wish, desire, p., 126:12 [O.E. *wȳscan*]

wyt, wytte: v., know, inf. and pres., 60:8, 68:4, 84:12; **wyst, wyste**: p., 57:6, 105:4, 115:5 [O.E. *witan*]

wytte: sb., mind, wit, 48:6, 157:3 [O.E. *witt*]

wytterly: adv., clearly, surely, 182:5 [O.N. *vitrliga*]

wyve: See **wife**

y: See **i**

yaf, yave: See **gefe**

yare: adj. and adv., ready, readily, 7:3, 9:10, 11:3, etc. [O.E. *gearo*]

yben, yblessed, yborn, y-bought: See **ben, boren, blessed, bey**

ybent: adj., bent, 42:2 [From O.E. v. *bendan*]

ycome, ycomen, ydo, ydon: See **come, don**

ye: a) sb., eye, 17:4, 28:11, 57:2, etc.; **yen**: pl., 96:2, 171:5, 173:2 [O.E. *ēage*]

b) also **yes**: adv., yea, yes, 69:1,4, 78:4, etc. [O.E *gēa*]

c) pers. pron., 2 pl. and polite address, subj. case, 2:12, 9:3, 14:1, etc.; **you, yow**: obl., 1:2, 4:2, 6:10, etc. [O.E.]

yede, yeden, yode: See **go**

yef, yefe, yeve, yf: a) conj., if, 21:11, 22:7, 25:5, etc. [O.E. *gif*]

b) See v. **geve**

yeld: v., repay, reward, p.part., 172:5; **yeldyst**: 2nd pers. sing. pres. ind., 170:8 [O.E. *gieldan*]

yen: See **ye**

yere: sb., year, 33:9, 103:10, 129:1, etc.; **yere, yeres**: pl., 5:4,7,10, etc. [O.E. *gēar*]

yfounde, ygo, yhold, yholde, yhote: See **find, go, hold, hete**

ylle: adv., badly; in expr. (he) liked ylle, (he) disliked, 52:2, 105:6 [O.N. *īllr*]

ylyght: See **light**

ynought: adv., enough, plenty of, 62:5 [O.E. *genōh*]

yode: See **go**

yonder: adv., yonder, over there, 100:11 [M.E.; cp M.L.G. *gender*]

yong, yonge: adj., young, 2:5, 7:4, 40:1, etc. [O.E. *geong*]

yoten: See **gete**

yplyght: See **plight**

ysene, yslayn, ytolde, ywent: See **se, sle, tell, go**

ywis, ywys, ywysse: See **iwisse**

Printed and bound by CPI Group (UK) Ltd, Croydon, CR0 4YY

13/04/2025

14656586-0005